W9-BUM-433

**PUNCH
ME UP
TO THE
GODS**

"*Punch Me Up to the Gods* obliterates what we thought were the limitations of not just the American memoir, but the possibilities of the American paragraph. I'm not sure a book has ever had me sobbing, punching the air, dying of laughter, and needing to write as much as Brian Broome's staggering debut. This shit is special."
— **Kiese Laymon, *New York Times* best-selling author of *Heavy***

"*Punch Me Up to the Gods* is some of the finest writing I have ever encountered and one of the most electrifying, powerful, simply spectacular memoirs I—or you—have ever read. And you *will* read it; you *must* read it. It contains everything we all crave so deeply: truth, soul, brilliance, grace. It is a masterpiece of a memoir and Brian Broome should win the Pulitzer Prize for writing it. I am in absolute awe and you will be, too."
— **Augusten Burroughs, *New York Times*
best-selling author of *Running with Scissors***

"*Punch Me Up to the Gods* is a pain-filled tour de force of incredible beauty. The writing is as exquisite as the story is at times horrific. A true work of art. Not *one* of the best new books I've read this year, but quite simply the best."
— **Sapphire, author of *Push* and *The Kid***

"*Punch Me Up to the Gods* feels like a scream at the end of a summit. It's what happens when one has had to climb a mountain of -isms in the dark, abandoning training and precedent, to find a singular freedom. One separate even from the freedom sold to us in . . . well, books. But Broome has shattered every rule and has come to make a mess of what we think of as family, Blackness, sexuality, and most importantly, the memoir. With unflinching honesty, he delivers a necessary testament of his refusal to allow the strangling expectations of life to rob him of his personhood. We should all hope to be this courageous, not only in our writing, but in our living."

— Jason Reynolds, *New York Times* best-selling
author of *Long Way Down* and *Look Both Ways*

"This book is light forged from darkness, in the way that James Baldwin's writing is or in the way that Barry Jenkins's *Moonlight* is but also in a way that is singular and vivid and wholly original. Brian Broome writes about the 'real America' we hear about so often — steel towns full of the forgotten working class — and the real America we rarely hear about — the Black folks, the queer folks, the Others in those spaces that push back against a narrative hellbent on erasing them. *Punch Me Up to the Gods* is furious and dazzling, poetic and gritty. It is vital for every type of reader and a gift to every reader who has had to fight to affirm their existence in this country."

— R. Eric Thomas, national best-selling
author of *Here for It* and *Reclaiming Her Time*

"In *Punch Me Up to the Gods*, Brian Broome breaks the rules, and in doing so, breaks our hearts and our minds wide open. He forces us to question what we think we know about the way narratives are constructed or who becomes a final authority. Memory carries its own weight in this work, the anchor drawing us back to what we already know but are retaught by experiencing Broome's bright and curious language. This thrilling debut sparkles with deft honesty and shakes alive something hiding deep in the night of our psyches."

— Camonghne Felix, author of *Build Yourself a Boat*

"I wish there was a way to teleport *Punch Me Up to the Gods* back to a twelve or a fifteen or even a twenty-five-year-old me to prove that the anxiety and pressure I felt to perform 'appropriate masculinity' wasn't singular. Brian Broome's remarkable memoir removes the veil from all of the performing, all of the acting, all of the preening, and just reveals, us — as flawed and as funny and as scared and as weird and as human as we can be. As we're supposed to be. But since time machines don't exist (yet), I'll settle for adult me reading Broome's hilarious and heat-seeking missile of a memoir and discovering a new-as-fuck way to write an old-as-fuck story."

— **Damon Young, author of**
What Doesn't Kill You Makes You Blacker

"Black, dark, queer, and poor. These are the vectors of *Punch Me Up to the Gods*. Brian Broome, literary son of the Black modernist giant Gwendolyn Brooks, writes from the center as one declared wrong among the wronged, one cast out of those cast aside, and one who desperately seeks tenderness. And on the hard road of growing up he finds wisdom, poetry, and love. This spectacular, unforgettable, and wholly innovative book is an ethical reckoning that tears us away from cruelty and invites us to witness real beauty."

— **Imani Perry, author of *Looking for Lorraine* and *Breathe***

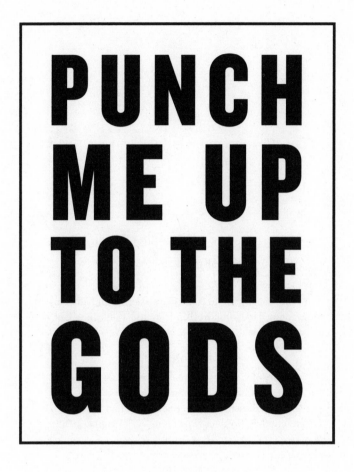

PUNCH ME UP TO THE GODS

BRIAN BROOME

Houghton Mifflin Harcourt
Boston   New York
2021

For information about permission to reproduce selections
from this book, write to trade.permissions@hmhco.com or to
Permissions, Houghton Mifflin Harcourt Publishing Company,
3 Park Avenue, 19th Floor, New York, New York 10016.

hmhbooks.com

Library of Congress Cataloging-in-Publication Data
Names: Broome, Brian, author.
Title: Punch me up to the gods / Brian Broome.
Description: Boston : Houghton Mifflin Harcourt, 2021.
Identifiers: LCCN 2020044745 (print) | LCCN 2020044746 (ebook) |
ISBN 9780358439103 (hardcover) | ISBN 9780358449782 | ISBN 9780358449843 |
ISBN 9780358439110 (ebook)
Subjects: LCSH: Broome, Brian. | African American authors — Biography. |
African American gay men — Biography.
Classification: LCC E185.97.B84 A3 2021 (print) | LCC E185.97.B84 (ebook) |
DDC 306.76/6208996073 — dc23
LC record available at https://lccn.loc.gov/2020044745
LC ebook record available at https://lccn.loc.gov/2020044746

Book design by Emily Snyder

Printed in the United States of America
1 2021
4500823073

"We Real Cool" by Gwendolyn Brooks from *Selected Poems*. Copyright ©
1963 by Gwendolyn Brooks. Reprinted by consent of Brooks Permissions.

The author has changed the names of some of the people portrayed in this book.

To Brother and Sister Outsiders everywhere.

CONTENTS

WE SING SIN

WE THIN GIN

WE JAZZ JUNE

WE DIE SOON

TABULA RASA

INTRODUCTION

by Yona Harvey

James Baldwin's gifts as a writer were evident and well documented by the time of his memorial service in New York City on December 8, 1987. On that day, Toni Morrison, Maya Angelou, and Amiri Baraka went on record to convey how Baldwin, as a man and as an artist, made them feel. Each of these legendary writers exalted Baldwin in their own way; but the common thread was one of feeling loved by Baldwin, of loving Baldwin as their brother, and, most essentially, of being seen by him. Baldwin, after all, was a mirror for Black artists, for Black intelligentsia, and for the everyday Black American experiences that would inspire generations to come. Morrison said in her tribute, which was excerpted later that month in the *New York Times Book Review,* "I have been seeing the world through your eyes for so long, I believed that clear, clear view was my own."

Indeed, Baldwin's vision impacted not only Morrison, but countless others who recognized themselves and their struggles in Baldwin's language. "We all react to and, to whatever extent, become what that eye sees," Baldwin wrote in "Freaks and the American Ideal of Manhood," for *Playboy* magazine in 1985. "This judgment," he continued, "begins in the eyes of one's parents (the crucial, the definitive, the all-but-everlasting judgment), and so we move, in the vast and claustrophobic gallery of Others, on up or down the line, to the eye of one's enemy or one's friend or one's lover." The fear of judgment Baldwin named is older than the Bible. Brian Broome's debut memoir, *Punch Me Up to the Gods,* brought this fear to the surface in riveting detail. I recognized in this book Broome's ability to hone that dreadful eying of our nonconformist behaviors, which were maligned as flawed and erroneous — whether wanting to stay inside and read rather than go outside and play, preferring dolls to trucks (or vice versa), or the genuine inability to *behave* as others insisted we do. This predicament was especially tough for those of us who knew our disobedience would have consequences ranging from the minor — our favorite things taken away for a period — to the major — being bullied, physically or verbally abused, or, in some instances, being kicked out of the house. *Punch Me Up to the Gods* reminded me that Baldwin's "vast and claustrophobic gallery of Others" was not often comprised of strangers, but of people in close proximity whose affections we coveted, of people who, for better or worse, we envied, admired, desired, relied upon, and frequently loved. We wanted to be loved beyond judgment, without having to conform. With tenderness, devilish wit, and the most gorgeous prose this side of the Ohio River, Broome renders these relational complexities as persistent and grounded, with few escape hatches, which make them difficult to dismiss.

As adults, the gallery's composition may change, but complex ideas of intersectionality, politics, race, gender, and identity risk being misunderstood, distorted, and outright falsified — even among artists. Even in chosen families, relationships can feel euphoric and everlasting at one point, only to feel combatant and fleeting in another. Consider James Baldwin and Richard Wright or Ishmael Reed and Amiri Baraka. Consider visual artist Faith Ringgold's infamous critique of her daughter Michele Wallace's book *Black Macho and the Myth of the Superwoman* and every Black critic and writer who weighed in on that intergenerational debate. *Punch Me Up to the Gods* reminded me that sometimes the trouble has less to do with the truthfulness of our multidimensional narratives, and more to do with "who pays what for speaking," as Audre Lorde put it.

Reading *Punch Me Up to the Gods* revealed that my concerns about judgment were also about nagging doubts and insecurities, Baldwin's "all-but-everlasting" hang-ups and imperfections, which I'd rather not expose publicly. As a young college student in the mid-to-late nineties, I must have absorbed some of the vitriol and backlash against memoir writing. I certainly recall being a poet in an MFA program, attending writers' conferences, and hearing disparaging words spoken about the so-called sham of creative nonfiction threatening the livelihoods of *real writers* and criticizing the genre's *godfather,* Lee Gutkind. People hated the word "creative," I'm guessing, because it implied for them something untrue or invented. The nineties did not seem to me a great time for folks to be all up in their feelings. Luckily, lasting literature has a way of bending time.

Punch Me Up to the Gods does this. Broome's unsentimental, unapologetic recollections of the past—some of them cringeworthy—liberate us to view our pasts as well. He is not a self-help or tour guide, but someone offering a portal to his hometown. Broome doesn't aim to coerce or convince us of anything. It is as if I was there too. But I have room to process for myself—without intrusion, without judgment. Reading this memoir was more like listening to Broome's stories on a drive in the dark in which the conversation ebbed and flowed, high and low. He revealed one disappointment or another and then, like a seasoned stand-up comedian, delivered the anodyne punch line, which made me think as much as laugh.

Broome doesn't wait for the materialization of the perfect self, which—spoiler alert—never happens. *Punch Me Up to the Gods* unearths the mysteries of Broome's longings and perceived shortcomings—the need to be accepted, to be loved, and to feel desired persists. It's that persistence, that sense of ongoingness that carried me page after page, like a good friend will do, leading with candor, sidesplitting humor, and charm. It's that ongoingness which made space for contradiction and error. Writing openly about growing up "dark-skinned" in Warren, Ohio, and feeling at odds with his body,

Broome opens the door to overlooked vulnerabilities, to a conversation about the hurts of colorism that seemed less prevalent in literature authored by Black men. *"If I'm a work-in-progress,"* it seems to say, *"then who am I to judge? I'll make space for you."* It says the damaging slights and wounds of racial discrimination, family secrets, and heartbreak need not be overcome completely in a single, tidy narrative. What a relief. Because would we even trust a book that claimed to do that?

In his foreword to *Romare Bearden: His Life and Art,* August Wilson recounts the day he stood outside Romare Bearden's Manhattan loft "daring myself to knock on his door." Wilson telegraphs his life-changing experience of encountering Bearden's work at the age of thirty-two and, twelve years earlier, Bessie Smith and the blues. It's an homage to Bearden, but also a testament to the power of art, its ability to challenge us, to transform our relationships, and to sharpen our perceptions of the communities in which we grew up: "I was, as are all artists, searching for a way to define myself in relation to the world I lived in. The blues gave me a firm and secure ground. It became, and remains, the wellspring of my art." The images in Bearden's exhibition catalog, *The Prevalence of Ritual,* helped Wilson translate the blues aesthetic to the narratives of his award-winning plays: "What for me had been so difficult, Bearden made seem so simple, so easy. What I saw was black life presented on its own terms, on a grand and epic scale, with all its richness and fullness. . . . I was looking at myself in ways I hadn't thought of before and have never ceased to think of since." The narrative Wilson aimed to produce was also inspired by Baldwin. For Wilson, that narrative was the one "that sustains black American life."

To that end, reading *Punch Me Up to the Gods* feels like assemblage—the remnants of internalized judgments and accumulated hurts quilted together. The humor and shamelessness offered warmth. Broome was that friend talking and laughing *too loudly* as some have accused us, but with a narrative completely uninhibited by the fear of outside critique. It's hard to imagine Baldwin

ever being out of fashion or criticized for similar examinations because, for so many of us, Baldwin never went away. But he was in
fact critiqued for positing "love" as one possible solution to politi-
cal upheaval. Eldridge Cleaver accused Baldwin of self-hatred. And
in a 1998 review of Baldwin's *Collected Essays,* edited by Toni Morrison, then *New York Times Book Review* editor Michael Anderson
scorned a "near-frenzied gratitude" for Baldwin's work in the early
1960s and in the 1990s which, in his estimation, suffered from an
unexamined nostalgia by readers of Henry Louis Gates' generation.
Even as a Black male editor, Anderson disparaged Baldwin's recurring themes of the troubled relationship between father and son
and American racism. According to Anderson, Baldwin had lost his
audience after 1964 because America had "moved forward." Consid-
ering the Black Lives Matter movement, however, Baldwin's skepti-
cism of America's racial progress seems more prescient.

Fortunately, a new generation of writers can seek and find themselves in print and digital platforms beyond the *New York Times* and
now in *Punch Me Up to the Gods,* which resists accusations like
Cleaver's and brings to mind again Baldwin's "vast and claustrophobic gallery of Others." For some of us, it manifested in a chant
heard whenever siblings or cousins disobeyed instructions to go to
the store and come right back, damaged the living room furniture,
spilled or broke something they had no business messing with: "You
gon get in trouble," we said—the last syllable of the word, trouble, drawn out several seconds. Before reading *Punch Me Up to the
Gods,* I hadn't thought about that singsong chant in years. "You gon
get in trouble," I whispered above the pages, as if I were seven years
old, fearing adult wrath and disapproval. Reading Broome's words
at first was like worrying about a favorite cousin getting yanked by
his neck because of a comment spoken too loudly, the too-true sen-
timent exasperating and embarrassing a parent or elder, though
they'd never admit it. As children, we knew there would be consequences for our alleged grievances. And in adulthood, there's fear
of the memories and, very often, of the telling and how we might

be judged. We are somehow expected to keep our hurts and short-comings private, even as they threaten to suffocate us. I didn't want Broome to "get in trouble," to be harshly judged. But I felt defiantly excited by the sheer audacity of what he wrote, the deceptive ease and shrug of it—not pained or confessional, just the facts of his life, that steady tension between content and delivery (often humorous), threading the bobbin of this incredible book.

Gwendolyn Brooks praised Baldwin because he "dared to confront and examine himself, ourselves, and the enigmas between," which is a skill of great artists and scholars. The Pulitzer Prize–winning poet also called Baldwin "love personified" in her formal introduction of him at the Library of Congress less than a year before Baldwin died. Would Baldwin have written more essays like "Freaks and the American Ideal of Manhood" if he felt he had permission? My own "frenzy" for Baldwin's work is, of course, for Baldwin's language and sentences, but also the content of those sentences, the flashes of the father bubbling to the surface, the prophetic readings of American hypocrisy, and the utter frustration with what poet Douglas Kearney has called "the changing same," riffing on Amiri Baraka's *Black Music* essay, "The Changing Same: R&B and New Black Music." Similarly, the themes in *Punch Me Up to the Gods* are timeless, undeniable, and, yes, recurring. It's the kind of writing for which we turn to nonfiction again and again.

What does Broome's eye see? There is something specific and tragic about that resegregated, 1980s Ohio locale—both physically and emotionally. Too much hinged on the whims of white people and their children. Even the ones who claimed to "like" you sometimes proved unreliable and disloyal—especially beyond the school grounds. Broome reminded me of the early frustrations of daring to trust others—especially of another class and race—and the hurt of having that trust trampled or betrayed in a region where creative and social outlets were so few, of the suffocating and limited choices for black expression. *Punch Me Up to the Gods* will take its well-earned place among the narratives of Black masculinity because it enriches and complicates those narratives through its art and through its refusal of Black macho stereotypes. It is written in the tradition of great nonfiction, but also with the fluidity and experimentation that contemporary memoirs and personal essays lend themselves to. This was a realm in which Baldwin flourished, though his critics didn't have a working language for what he was doing. *Punch Me Up to the Gods* offers a new way of seeing what will influence Black readers and writers for many years to come.

Black artists and scholars have relied upon and been sustained by literary conversations across decades. Steven G. Fullwood, founder of the Schomburg Center for Research in Black Culture's In the Life Archive, understood the importance of coming-out books being published each year. Every generation possesses its unique variations of ease or difficulty in so doing. In an interview with Sheena C. Howard, he also notes that despite the Schomburg having a huge collection of queer life materials in poetry (no shortage there) and fiction (gaining on the poetry), the nonfiction works were lacking. He recognized trends in publishing and archival preservation and tracked what was missing. The "explosion of culture" and queer organizations in the 1960s and '70s was crucial, though Fuller found that "nobody knew about them unless you lived in New York or Philadelphia or DC or somewhere out in California or possibly Atlanta."

Like Broome, naivety and optimism landed me in Pittsburgh. As a writer of Not–New York and Not-California, I cherish Broome's attention to Black life in the overlooked parts of the Midwest and regions like Pittsburgh, where we have managed to write and mature as artists. Pittsburgh native August Wilson ultimately never knocked on Bearden's door. But his ten plays known as the *Century Cycle* are a testament to Bearden's work and the ability of artists to commune across time and space through their creations. They affirm the notion that no matter where we escape, the imprints of our birthplaces and hometowns shape up. These imprints and all of the regrets and longings accompanying them have sparked some of the most memorable and lasting works. *Punch Me Up to the Gods* is written with that same spark. Broome's memoir revisits the hurts, hilarities, and discomforts of coming out in imperfect Ohio, the temporary rest after narrow escape. I'm grateful for his friendship and for his watchful eye, the one aimed not only at the absurdities of others, but the one turned inward at his ongoing self. When reading *Punch Me Up to the Gods,* the impulse wasn't to compare Broome and Baldwin. The feeling, rather, was one of joy for readers and writers in the life expanding with this book in their hands. The feeling is one of joy in acknowledging Baldwin's legacy and Broome's inheritance—one, perhaps, neither writer could ever have imagined.

PUNCH ME UP TO THE GODS

We Real Cool

THE POOL PLAYERS.
SEVEN AT THE GOLDEN SHOVEL.

We real cool. We
Left school. We

Lurk late. We
Strike straight. We

Sing sin. We
Thin gin. We

Jazz June. We
Die soon.

— GWENDOLYN BROOKS

THE INITIATION OF TUAN

I am standing at a bus stop in McKeesport, Pennsylvania, on the Black end of town. It's a hot but overcast summer day. To my left is a young man mesmerized by his cell phone. He laughs out loud periodically while staring into its depths, then his thumbs fly like hummingbird wings over the keyboard. He is dressed like all the other young men around here, in the newest iteration of "distressed" jeans, with stark white tennis shoes and a shirt with a sports logo emblazoned across the front. I notice him only because a little boy wearing an almost identical outfit in miniature is circling around and around his feet like a toy train. The toddler, who is doing all the things toddlers do with their newly found feet, pitches forward with full force onto the sidewalk, enormous toddler head first. The women around me gasp and so do I. Some of them take halting steps toward the boy. Pearls are clutched while we wait for the young man, who I assume is the boy's father, to pick the boy up and tend to him. The boy's wails are high-pitched and earsplitting.

The child's name is Tuan.

"Shake it off, Tuan," the young father says, glancing briefly down at the boy and then turning back to his phone. Tuan sits down on the sidewalk only to howl more loudly. The women around me shift their eyes from the child to the father and back again. Their worried looks are digging deep creases between their brows. They exchange disapproving glances with one another. The boy's screams are now rattling his voice box and his mouth is open so wide that his little face appears to be tearing itself apart.

As I watch the boy sitting on the sidewalk, I try to remember what *real* crying feels like. I can't. I can only remember the tactics I employed to try to suppress it.

Tuan's father picks the boy up off the ground and places him on the bus stop bench before turning back to the flickering lights inside his phone. Tuan has no interest in shaking it off.

"Be a man, Tuan," the boy's father says out of the corner of his mouth, eyes steady on the phone. Tuan has no interest in being a man, and his screaming continues. Tuan's father kneels down, grips the boy by the shoulders, and looks him straight in the eyes.

"Stop cryin', Tuan! Be a man, Tuan!"

When I was a boy, I used to sit on the back steps of our house after an ass-whuppin' because, afterward, I was always commanded not to leave our yard. My father would wander out after a long while with his head down and the same hands he'd used to just whoop my ass shoved deeply into his pockets. Instead of letting the screen door slam as he usually did, he would close it carefully. He knew he had let his temper get the best of him and so he would come out, weighed down by a remorse he was unable to express with words. He'd just sit down next to me and quietly look off into the distance. He'd fish out his packet of Winstons, place one between his lips, use both hands on his lighter to light it, and exhale a thick cloud of ivory smoke. For a little while, he and I would share a silence that was occasionally broken by my hiccupping sobs and sharp intakes of air. Sometimes he would come out bearing gifts: a Popsicle or a candy bar that he'd hand to me wordlessly while still looking out on the back yard. And we'd sit there until he couldn't take listening to my sopping-wet whimpering any longer, and he'd command me suddenly as if he'd just woken out of a dream.

"Stop cryin'. You done cried enough. Stop cryin' right now."

I would stop immediately.

As Tuan's father's voice becomes louder, demanding that the boy stop crying, all I want to do is pick the boy up to make sure he's alright. I can't explain it. Something to do with his tiny shoulders being held in a vise-like grip by the very person he needs tenderness from in this moment. Something about the unaddressed ache.

And I realize that this, what I am witnessing, is the playing out of one of the very conditions that have dogged my entire existence: this "being a man" to the exclusion of all other things.

As Tuan's father publicly chastises him for his tears, I remember how my own tears were seen as an affront. I remember how my own father looked at me as if I was leaking gasoline and about to set the whole concept of Black manhood on fire.

Stop crying. Be a man.

My father's beatings were like lightning strikes. Powerful, fast, and unpredictable. He held his anger so tightly that, when it finally overtook him, the force was bone-shaking. He punched me like I was a grown-ass man. He went blind with rage and just punched with all the strength of a steelworker. It never took more than one to lay me on my back, windless. Then he would dare me to get up. I never did. When he punched me in the stomach, my flesh engulfed his fist. When he caught me in the chest, I could swear I heard ribs crack. His punches to my head rocked it back on my shoulders so violently that I momentarily lost vision in one eye. This is how he meted out punishment for the offenses of not listening to him, for talking too slick, or for "acting like a girl."

I close my eyes at the memory and, in my mind, drop down to Tuan's perspective. I see things through his eyes. I am looking into the angry face of the man who will teach me how to be in the world. I cannot understand his words, but I can see his furrowed brow and feel his hands imploring me to stop feeling what I am most definitely feeling. Stop feeling fear and pain. Tuan's father is telling me to tuck it away somewhere where no one can see it. To be ashamed of it. It's the age-old conundrum. Black boys have to be tough but, in doing so, we must also sacrifice our sensitivity, our humanity. I can feel his urgency and know that my body has done something wrong.

Tuan's wailing begins to subside, like a police siren fading into the distance, until he is silent. When he is, his father stands up, turns away, and begins once again to gaze into his phone. But back on the bench the boy's face is still contorted into a mask of pain and confusion. His lips are stretched out over his teeth and no sound dares escape his mouth. His breath comes in short bursts. His whole body is occupied with the act of suppressing. Fists clenched. Body taut. Eyebrows knitted in total concentration. He sits this way until the bus arrives and his father stands him on his feet.

I board the bus behind them as I'm drawn back to my boyhood lessons in disaffectedness, nonchalance, and hollow strength. It was a never-ending performance that I could not keep up to save my life. And when I failed consistently, there was never any shortage of people around to punish me for it.

WE REAL COOL

COLDER

Whatever *it* was, I already knew by ten years old that I didn't have it.

I couldn't access it. Couldn't summon it. Couldn't fake it. But the boys all around me had it in spades, this elusive quality that only Black boys could possess. White boys didn't have it. Whenever they tried to pretend that they did, it came off forced, stiff, and rehearsed. When they tried to be "cool," you could see right through them. I didn't possess this quality either and I knew of no way to make it come to me. It's a trait that defies verbiage and the only thing I could understand about it at the time was that it seemed to involve an almost superhuman ability to lean on things. Up against buildings and telephone poles and cars, not giving a shit about the thing upon which you are leaning. Nor should you appear worried about that thing shifting under your weight to send you crashing to the ground. It seemed to hinge on the absolute belief that whatever you were casually leaning up against would support you, because you, after all, are *you*.

I learned what white boys do, and what Black boys are supposed to do to counter it at the foot of the master: my best friend, Corey. When we were ten years old, we sat in his bedroom after school surrounded by his baseball, basketball, and football equipment as he admonished me. The differences between Black boys and white boys, he explained, are vast and it is entirely up to the Black boy to make those differences clear. White boys could just do whatever. But Black boys had to show through our behavior that we were undeniably, incontrovertibly the most male. The toughest.

We sat on either end of his bed and I got lost in his pretty brown eyes as he explained that white boys were basically girls — "pussies" — and that there was nothing worse than a boy being like a girl. I stared blankly, wanting to kiss him. According to him, the seemingly simple act of being white and male made one "soft" and a "punk," but Black boys were constructed of special stuff that made us stronger, colder, *cooler*. All I wanted to do was hold his hand. But I listened because he was beautiful. He was light-skinned with curly black hair and straight, white teeth. He was the polar opposite of me, too dark-skinned with the teeth in my head crawling all over each other like they were trying to escape a house on fire. He talked on as I got lost in his face.

"White folks," he explained, "won't let you do anything anyways, so you gotta show 'em. All they do is fuck wit Black folks all the time, so you gotta prove to 'em that you won't be fucked with right from the start. That's why white dudes be scared of us, because they know that, when it get right down to it, we cooler. That's why they women always come for our dick."

I didn't understand any of this. Corey explained that the rules were simple. There were girl things and there were boy things and white boys liked girl things and acting like a white boy or a girl of any color was prohibited. The list of "girl things" included: studying, listening, being "pussy-whipped," and curiosity. There were categories and subcategories, but being pussy-whipped was the worst of these transgressions. Corey explained that Black boys were to always be in control of girls.

There were no gray areas and, each time I visited his home, he scolded me about how he'd heard I'd messed up that day at school. He never interacted with me in public. He called me "white boy" and doled out punishments for my behavior that were severe. He "play punched" me to toughen me up—blows to the side of my head or in the arm that were so hard that I knew somewhere deep down inside that he really didn't like me at all. Our "play wrestling" moved from play to real rapidly, like a switch had been flipped inside him. He bloodied my nose many times. He split my lips against my crooked teeth and once locked me in a port-o-potty by eliciting the help of other boys to lean on the door from the outside. The injuries that I sustained from him were dismissed by the adults as a result of "wrastling" or playing like horses. He wasn't whupping my ass, really. He was pummeling the girl out of me. I took his disguised ass-whuppin's almost every day, believing that, one day, he would deliver the one punch that might change me.

I didn't know where Corey's father was. It never came up and something told me not to ask. He lived with his mother and there were times when I wanted to tell on him. But she treated him as a crowned prince who could do no wrong and, the one time I tried, I was only asked accusingly "Well, what did you do to *him*?" and then admonished for being a "tattletale," which as near as I could tell was a girly attribute.

The house was his. He had full dominion. He had all the new toys and his own stereo. His clothes seemed to be perpetually new. The denim of his blue jeans was always that rich, deep shade of royal blue, rolled up at the cuff to reveal the lighter shade of blue underneath. Unlike me in my old and dingy clothes, Corey was always fresh and his clothes fit him perfectly. He treated his mother like a servant and talked to her in a brazen and dictatorial way. He once told her to shut up, and I was left awestruck as I waited in vain for her to go upside his head like my mother would have with me. But all she did was shut up. I had never seen a Black boy with such power. He was a force in his house. He had the biggest say-so. I wanted to be him.

When I arrived at his house on a Saturday, I let myself in and stomped the snow from my boots. That winter was especially brutal. I was sent to his house by my parents every weekend and I mostly dreaded it. Whole days with him were a merciless trial. He was unpredictable. Moody. He called me poor and ugly. I never felt good when I left his house, nursing a Corey-inflicted wound that I chose to hide from my parents later. But my father was concerned about how many girls I was playing with on a regular basis. I was sent to Corey as a form of therapy. My father loved him and would clap him hard on the back whenever he came around, and they would laugh. I wanted that from my father too and believed that Corey could fix me. I didn't mind that much if every once in a while, that fixing resulted in a fat lip. I knew that he was the epitome of cool. Everyone did. I was grateful that he was my friend, and, for some reason, I felt he needed me as much as I needed him.

After I stomped the snow from my boots, I removed my jacket, scarf, and hat and hung them on the coatrack by the front door. I walked down the hallway past the living room, where his mother was in her seemingly perpetual position in a lounge chair mindlessly doing crochet and staring at the television.

"Hi, Brian."

His mother said this vacantly and with no enthusiasm, not so much reacting to my arrival as she was to the sound of the door opening and closing. I walked to Corey's closed bedroom door and hesitated, listening to him doing some sort of karate on himself on the other side. I took a deep breath and knocked lightly twice. The door flew open.

He didn't even give me time to step inside before he grabbed my elbow, pushing me backward toward the very rack upon which I had just hung my hat and coat. He was fully dressed to go out into the snow. I didn't want to go back out, but there was no time for argument. He was in a rush. Seized by some sort of urgency. He explained to his mother quickly that we were going outside to play. He hissed "Hurry up!" at me from between clenched teeth and his mother looked up absently from her crochet to the window at the blinding snow coming down in drifts and then back at us with incredulity. I wanted her to tell him that we couldn't go, but then her face went blank and she returned to the mess of yarn on her lap. When I was fully dressed again, Corey all but shoved me out the front door, and it was only when we were a safe distance from his house that he began to explain.

"Everybody callin' you white."

"What? Who?"

We were walking through the field behind his mother's house and the snow was coming down so heavily that my face was already wet. Our footsteps were synchronized so that the deep snow under our feet crunched at the exact same time in a rhythm that made me feel as though he and I were actually friends. We headed toward the woods. The sky was the color of concrete and the branches of the trees were stripped naked of their leaves and heavy with snow. When we were deep into the woods and surrounded by them on all sides, Corey spoke again.

"Everybody. They say you act like a white boy and a fag and I told them you don't. I stood up for you. But they don't believe me, so we goin' to meet a girl."

"What girl?"

"Some girl. You gon' fuck her."

Corey explained that a council of Black boys in the neighborhood had met up and the topic had turned to why I was coming to his house on weekends. They knew, and he didn't like that. Corey's honor was at stake. He now had skin in the game. They had discussed such subtopics as how I was basically a white boy and a punk, and how I had failed to display the proper balance of nonchalance and boisterousness appropriate for a boy. They discussed my cursed bookishness; my disinterest and ineptitude at sports; my inability to lean against buildings, telephone poles, and cars; and the fact that I played with girls. In short, I was just not cool. It had been suggested that, by having kept company with me, Corey was a faggot by association. This could not stand. And now I was being taken to go fuck "some girl" to prove that Corey had not been hanging out with a sissy. I was to prove that I was not an insult to my race and my gender.

We marched through the snow until we arrived at the abandoned barn behind a neighbor's house. It was more of a garage, really, but had the look of an old barn that had fallen into disrepair. The pit of my belly was alive with fear and confusion.

Corey walked in ahead of me. The inside of the barn was scarred by graffiti and smelled of hay and motor oil. Car parts were scattered around an old, rusting dinosaur of a truck. They were mostly older boys. They were throwing rusty nuts and bolts at one another and laughing—until we walked in, and they froze. Each face was expectant and grinning. This group of nappy-headed, older boys I recognized from the neighborhood and from basketball courts and baseball diamonds that I had walked by quickly. There was only one face that I didn't recognize. I knew immediately that she was a project girl.

In my experience, project girls always came in one of two flavors: rambunctious and loud or withdrawn and silent. She seemed to be the latter, standing there impassively watching the boys behave like boys and wearing a pink jacket that was far too light for the weather. Her clothes were dingy apart from the hot pink of her wrap, and her hair was twisted into two haphazard cornrows at the very top of her head that had curled themselves upward, giving her the look of having antennae. She was bucktoothed and skinny and her demeanor was at once bored and disassociated. She seemed resigned to what she had to do and, when she looked at me, her eyes fixed with the knowledge that I was to be the one this time. Her hooded jacket with the soiled white trim hung off one shoulder. She seemed older, maybe eleven or twelve, wearing highwater jeans and a dirty yellow T-shirt. Five boys surrounded her, each blowing plumes of steam from their mouths and noses. She just looked me up and down like she was about to stamp my passport: unimpressed and barely interested. After she was done here, she would get whatever candy or potato chips these boys had promised her and that was all she seemed interested in. Her nonchalance was an indication that she already knew boys were just something she had to endure in order to get ahead. She was already accustomed to the idea that, in this life, much like a building or a telephone pole or a car, her purpose was to be leaned on by boys.

Corey marched me toward her like he was giving away the bride and the boys all circled around to get a better look. The barn fell silent for half a second.

"Y'all told me he was light-skinned."

Her disappointment was total. The boys giggled, and there was another moment of silence. I had no idea what to do. I didn't know what was expected. Then Corey told her to take down her pants and she did. They fell around her ankles, and then all the boys in a chorus of slithering whispers told me to take my dick out. Some of their voices hadn't changed yet, so I heard the command in different pitches all insisting that I do it and do it now. I looked to see all their wide eyes trained lasciviously on my fly. The girl took my hand and slowly put it on her new and hard breast. I wanted to run. Everybody here knew what was supposed to be happening except for me, so I did what I was told. I undid my fly and belt and my pants dropped to my ankles. The frigid air rinsed my legs. I slid my underwear down and they hovered on my calves just above my trousers. No answers came to me. No instinct gripped me. My penis just hung there, stubby, dumb, useless, and getting cold.

The girl was irritated. She stepped toward me and I stood stock-still, looking her directly in her distant eyes. She smelled like dirt and perfume. She arched her back a little, reached her arms around to grab my butt and thrust the warmth of her thighs against mine and then started to move her hips slowly and the boys went wild with whisper-shouting. She breathed hot into my ear.

"This how," she said.

And I just stood there with my fingers clenched into fists at the end of my stiff arms as she moved warm skin back and forth across my cold and oblivious penis. Each time she thrust her hips, the boys got louder and louder until the barn was alive with the echoes of catcalls from the mouths of boys who had just learned how to apply the word "fuck" practically.

And then it was over.

It was only over because she got tired of doing it. There had been minimal response from me. I tried to grab her by the shoulders to kiss her like I'd seen on TV. She blocked my hands, snatched her head away, and looked at me with a quizzical anger, as if I had tried to slap her across the face. The girl looked up at the boys who were, by this point, bored and fully disappointed by my performance. She jerked away from me quickly and announced "I gotta get home or I'mma be in trouble." Then she pulled up her pants, flipped the hood up on her coat, zipped it, and headed for the barn door, taking most of the boys with her. They all ran past me without a word as I stood there with my pants still around my ankles.

So, this was fucking.

I felt sick. I knew that this was what my mother was talking about when she derided people for being "nasty" and now I was such a person. Corey turned around from giving his high-fives to exiting boys as I was zipping up. He was silent for a moment.

"You didn't do it right. You s'posed to get it in there. You s'posed to gitcha dick in there." I didn't understand what he was talking about.

When we exited the barn, I turned left to follow him back to his house. He stopped me. He told me that it wasn't cool that I didn't get it in there and then hit me with a punch in the chest so hard that I doubled over in pain. I could feel the resentment behind it. I could feel the hate.

He turned abruptly and began to walk back toward the woods. I stood there for a while until he disappeared into them. I knew that I shouldn't try to visit him anymore. I walked slowly away from the barn toward my house, trying to think of lies to tell my father about why Corey and I weren't friends anymore. The snow began to fall faster, like rain.

I felt the pain of his very last punch all the way back home.

I step into the aisle of the bus behind Tuan and his father, remembering the times my father tried to warn me about the world. I remember how he tried to make me listen, telling me that I needed a thicker skin and how he'd rather kill me himself than see white people do it. I was a clay that he molded, not with fingers but with punches. My father told me that man was made in God's image and that it was my duty to live up to that image.

But my Black, male body has betrayed its manhood on many occasions. My hips have swung too freely, and my heart has allowed itself to be broken far too easily. Tears, by far, have been my most pernicious traitors, and it took a long time before I was able to dry the wellspring up. My body has finally learned.

Out on the back steps, after my ass-whuppin's, I sat in anticipation of the few seconds when my father would be gentle with me. I liked these moments even as the side of my face pulsated with pain. I secretly loved his broad hand on my back and the brief but soft drumming motion of his fingers. "Stop cryin'. You done cried enough now."

I wanted him to be this way all the time, but I only had a limited amount of time before tenderness turned once again to anger. My father back then believed in beating Black boys the way Black boys are supposed to be beaten. For our own good, he would say.

Meant to toughen us up for a world where white people feed off our pain and to teach us that we cannot give them the satisfaction. Any Black boy who did not signify how manly he was at all times deserved to be punched back up to God to be remade, reshaped. Sometimes I would look up into his face after my ass-whuppin' and I could feel the apology radiating off of him. But he would never apologize because he wanted to teach me that the world wouldn't.

On the bus, Tuan and his father sit at the front, in the sideways seats facing the aisle. I choose a forward-facing seat across the aisle from them and place my oversized suitcase underneath and rest my feet on it. I tell myself that my seat choice is random, that I want to look out the window, but I know better. I sit here because I want a good view. I want to watch them. There's something I want to see.

The boy has stopped crying completely and has moved on to an entirely new mood with the movement of the vehicle now to distract him. He is chattering nonstop; pointing to various items out the window, babbling with all the enthusiasm of a child, and tugging at his father who is now talking on the phone. His father silences him. "Tuan, chill out, man."

I am picturing my own father from my earliest memories. I can just vaguely recall a time when he seemed to like me. I remember riding on his shoulders around our backyard and his early attempts to play with me. I remember him throwing me up in the air and those few seconds in time when I was weightless, giggling, and thrilled, with no doubt whatsoever that he would catch me. But there were times when he didn't. There were times when the joke was to let me fall to the ground. Never hard enough to get hurt, but just hard enough for me to remember.

I hear Tuan's father trying to calm the boy down once again.

"Be quiet, Tuan. I'm on the phone."

Be cool, Tuan. Be cool.

There are so few people on the bus that I can witness their every interaction, or lack thereof. I clearly hear the voice of the woman Tuan's father is now talking to on speakerphone. She sounds angry. Fed up. Tuan's father is giving as good as he's getting. Telling her that she's crazy in various and colorful ways and when he's finally had enough, he succinctly pushes a button to end the call, in the middle of her sentence.

The boy hasn't noticed this spectacle. He is standing on the seat facing toward the window, watching the world whizz by. This makes my muscles tense as the bus sways and makes short stops, and my body is readying itself to catch him should he go flying. His father looks away from his phone long enough to take in the boy's precarious position on the seat. He yells.

"Siddown!"

Tuan recognizes this serious tone and begins to turn around, but the bus hits a pothole, which slows his progress. His father grabs him by his arm, using it to force him into a seated position. Tuan takes this in stride. He sits at the seat's edge and lets his little legs dangle. He looks around the bus for something he can get into.

I am supposed to be minding my own business. I reach for the magazine in my backpack that I carry with me as a prop to put off people who cannot mind their own business. I glower at Tuan's father from beneath hooded eyes. I have decided that I hate him.

A woman boards, pays her fare, and sits directly across from the man and his boy. She and Tuan are now facing each other and she is immediately swept away. She smiles at the child and he covers his face in that shy way that little children do when they want to pretend to be shy. She waves at him using only her fingers and the boy giggles. This catches his father's attention and he looks up at the woman who addresses him, smiling.

"He is just *too cute!*"

Tuan's father looks down at the boy who is still covering his face. The father is now smiling as well. Proud. He removes the boy's chubby hands from his eyes and tells him to say hello to the nice lady.

"Hi, cutie!" the woman says. "What's his name?"

"You gonna tell her your name?"

The boy says nothing and turns his head sharply to the right to avoid eye contact.

"His name Tuan."

The woman is trying to maneuver so that she is looking into the boy's eyes.

"Hi, Tuaaaaaan! Are you out here breakin' hearts? You gonna break some little girl's heart someday?"

His father is pleased by this. "Yeah," he responds before he runs his fingers roughly through the boy's hair. The woman laughs heartily.

And now I hate her too.

I can only tell myself that it has already begun for this Black boy. I am witnessing it. I am watching the whole world ready itself to tell him about all the things that he cannot be.

Tuan and the lady start up a game of peekaboo and then he wants to show her that he knows his ABCs. He wants to show off how smart he is. He doesn't know them all, only up to "E." He sings them to the tune that we all learned to sing them. "A-B-C-D-E, A-B-C-D-E."

I struggle with a memory from a time long ago when I wanted to show everybody how smart I was.

The lady places her palm on her chest and giggles at Tuan's cuteness.

"A-B-C-D-E," Tuan chirps in the high register of a child's voice over and over again. Ten times in a row. Twenty? I lose track.

The memory won't back down. My boyhood, now fully stirred, comes hurrying back, clear as day.

"A-B-C-D-E," Tuan continues.

"F," I want to whisper, only to him. "The next letter is F."

I want to help the boy so badly I nearly say it out loud. But instead, I lean back in my seat, place my head against the window, and allow my twelve-year-old self to step up and tell his story.

WE LEFT SCHOOL

BEE

October 9, 1982

My name is Brian and I am in the sixth grade.

I don't really know how I got here. How did I end up standing on a stage in the school gym about to spell words?

There was a movie for the whole school in this very same gym last Friday and I got thrown out. You were supposed to have paid three dollars beforehand and have a permission slip signed by your parents in order to be here, but I was too scared to ask my mother for the money. I listen to her when she talks on the phone to the neighbor lady about how we don't have any.

My father doesn't have a job and lays around like a moldy dishrag all day. He isn't so much my father anymore as he is just a presence in the house; one that should be avoided, and you shouldn't go near or bother for any reason. He stays in their bedroom all day since he was laid off from the steel mill and, as far as I know, he doesn't do much. This is another thing my mother tells the neighbor lady on the phone. He sometimes comes out to float toward the refrigerator like a loose balloon, and then he goes back to the bedroom to deflate.

In this same gym last Friday, I snuck into the movie. I didn't pay the three dollars but thought that, with the whole school in here on folding chairs and in the bleachers, I wouldn't get caught. The movie was a treat for us here at LaBrae Middle School. Our school is mostly white and the white kids talk bad about the Black kids all day long. About how we're stupid and ugly and poor and how we don't have fathers. I get mad at that because I see my father every day.

The movie was *Popeye* with Robin Williams and it came out a few years ago in the real movie theaters. Robin Williams plays Popeye and he also plays Mork from Ork on TV and what I got to see of the movie was pretty good, but I haven't been to many movies. They raised a giant screen in here right in front of the stage where I'm sitting now and there was even free popcorn and the smell of it was all in the air. When they turned the lights out and pulled the shades down, it was as dark as a real movie theater in here and then I *knew* that I wouldn't get caught.

The last movie I went to see at a real movie theater was a long time ago. Two years ago, on my tenth birthday. It was a cartoon about a dog, and I felt way too old for it. But I had fun anyway. This was back when my father worked and our family had some money, and, for my birthday, my mother took me and my older sister to see the cartoon dog movie. My brother is also older and wasn't interested in the movie or my birthday.

My mother let me and my sister get whatever we wanted from the refreshment stand and then she sat a few rows behind us so that me and my sister could feel like we were adults. But it was a baby movie. I wanted to see a movie again so, last week, I sank down into one of the metal folding chairs they put out. I thought I was home free. Last week was not a good week.

They have taken down the movie screen now and got rid of the folding chairs. The whole gym is roaring with noise mixed with the occasional squeak of tennis shoes against the shiny floorboards. Earlier this morning, my teacher, Miss Biviano, told us there was going to be a school-wide spelling bee in the gym. That's how I ended up here. Looking out from the stage, I see students from the fifth to the eighth grades all crammed into the bleachers and some are sitting on the floor.

I see Miss Biviano pointing and yelling at a few students to sit down, which makes the meat dangling from her arm jiggle. She is a fat woman. Short and mean with a lazy eye that always confuses the class because you can't tell who she's actually talking to. You never know if she has caught you fooling around during quiet reading time or if she's caught the person two seats down from you fooling around during quiet reading time. If she doesn't yell out a person's name, it makes us all look around like she called the Lotto number and we're all trying to figure out who has the winning ticket. Her eye is everywhere at once so it's just easier to assume that she's yelling at you. She doesn't like me. She accuses me of cheating all the time and tells me that I have a "smart mouth" and that I use words that I shouldn't know. She took me out in the hallway once to ask me who writes my English homework for me and when I told her that I write it myself, I couldn't tell if she was looking into my eyes or over my head when she called me a liar. Sometimes, she makes me wonder myself if I *am* cheating.

My sister got a diary for her birthday two years ago and she didn't want it, so she just gave it to me. I filled it up pretty quick, so now I just use notebooks. I want to tell Miss Biviano that I write in my notebooks almost every day, but I don't think it would make a difference. She still always looks at me like I'm about to cause trouble.

I don't think she likes Black people because Black kids give her a hard time. Black boys are always a disruption in class and the Black girls are too loud and bossy, so I try not to be like them and blend into the background. But she doesn't treat me any better.

I was liking the movie in here last week until I saw Mr. Nye, the assistant principal, creeping around in the dark. I could tell by the way he walked that he was looking for the students who hadn't paid the three dollars so he could snatch them out one by one like weeds. He walked around with his head held high snapping it back and forth like a prairie dog that just popped out of a hole. Sniffing the air. I knew he was coming for me. I sank lower in my metal chair. I hoped that, even if he did see me, he wouldn't embarrass me over it. He did.

When he found me, he stood in front of me blocking my view with his hands on his hips. He didn't say anything. Just motioned with his hand for me to get up and follow him. We both knew why he was there. I left my popcorn on the seat. He didn't take any other students out of the movie. I guess I was the only one there who hadn't paid. I walked out tripping over the feet of seated kids who I could hear giggling. When we got into the hallway, he looked down at me with his pointy face and told me to go to room 209. When I got there, I joined the rest of the kids who didn't have three dollars. It was mostly other Black kids. The boys all looked up and laughed pointing fingers at me when I walked through the door. They said that the fact that I even wanted to go to the movie at all was corny. I never know what not to do. It's like they have a Black boy rule book that they won't show me, and I always end up doing the wrong thing, so I mostly try not to do anything at all. I sat as far away from them as possible because they all really hate me and think that I am a fag, which is a boy who likes other boys, but I know that I'm not one because I hate other boys. All they do is pick on you and laugh at you.

The teacher who was supposed to be in charge of room 209 had given up completely. She just sat at her desk staring out the window dreaming of a better job while the boys pretty much did whatever they wanted.

The other Black boys at my school always be in trouble. Misbehaving and talking back. They don't do their homework, fail every test, and the older ones spend all their time trying to kiss white girls. All these things are terrible, but especially the kissing part. They're all trying to be boyfriends with white girls and that makes the white girls have to be sneaky. I see it all the time. If a white girl gets caught with a Black boy, that makes the white boys not want to talk to her or be around her at all. They call her a slut. But the white girls like the attention from Black boys when there are no other white people around to see. They don't think of me that way, though. They like the Black boys who play football and basketball and run track like my brother. I see eighth-grade white girls and Black boys snuggled up into corners of empty hallways between classes smiling up in each other's faces all the time. Then the bell rings and they have to run and pretend like they don't know each other. The white girls don't want to be called "slut" and I can't blame them. This makes life hard for me because I don't want people to think I want to be with a white girl too. I don't care about white girls like that. I can't understand what all the fuss is about. They're okay as friends I guess, but all I know about them is that they spoiled and get whatever they want and cuss a lot.

I know that it's the eighties and everything, but I don't think that white people should be dating Black people. It's not what God wants. He made white people and Black people and meant for us to stick to our own kind. My school knows this rule. The whites and the Blacks are kept separate to stop the mixing. Nobody really says that out loud, but we do everything pretty much separately except when we are in classes together. The way it looks to me, white girls and Black girls are allowed to be friends but they never are. Black boys and white boys are allowed to be friends if they play sports together. White boys and Black girls ignore each other unless they are fighting. Black boys and white girls are not allowed to be friends for any reason. You'll get in trouble. But today Miss Biviano told me to sit onstage with a bunch of white girls and spell words and everyone, including me, knows that there must be some sort of mistake.

I guess it's luck. Maybe I cheated? I don't know that I know how to spell any better than anyone else. But I ended up in the top ten sixth graders yesterday after we had a mini spelling bee in our class. I didn't mean to do it. I didn't know this was going to happen. But I really love words. I love learning new ones. I love to write, and someday I will show my notebooks to someone. When I hear a word, it just appears in my head all lined up in order because I've seen it on pages before when I read. When I don't know a word, I look it up and then I use the thesaurus my auntie gave me to find different words that mean the same thing. There's nothing special about that.

We're going to be starting the spelling bee soon. I just saw Mr. Nye stand up and head toward the stage. Jodie Henderson is one of the white girls up here with me and this makes me nervous. She is the smartest person in our class. I am the only Black person on the stage. This makes things worse.

Mr. Nye hates me even more than Miss Biviano does. He's a skinny little pigeon-toed white man with a little bit of power, a balding head, and a pinched face. He wears short-sleeved polyester dress shirts, polyester ties, and polyester pants. He is practically made of polyester. I am the only Black boy that he's not nice to at school, as far as I can tell. He seems to get along okay with all the others because they are all on the sports teams and I am not on any. He jokes around with them and slaps them on the back. But he watches me real close like he knows something about me that I don't even know. Sometimes, I'll catch him when I'm sitting in the cafeteria eating my lunch. I'll look up and see him standing there leaning against the wall with his arms folded, staring at me like he wants to punch me in the face right then and there. When I look at him, he doesn't look away. He just keeps staring, taking big bites out of a pear that he pulls from his polyester pocket. When I look down at my lunch tray, I can still feel him looking at me. He doesn't like that some of my friends are white girls, I think.

He did help me in baseball once, though.

My father made me join the pee wee baseball team and I was so bad that he just stopped coming to the games. My mother kept coming, though. She held on to that mother-hope that just seems silly after a while. Every time I stepped up to the plate, I embarrassed myself. The rest of the team groaned out loud in the dugout when it was my turn at bat. Some of the parents even groaned. But I could hear my mother in the stands yelling for me.

"C'mon, Brian!" and "You can do it, Brian!"

Her cheering was useless. I dragged the bat behind me when I walked up to the plate knowing full well what was about to happen. Just ready to get it over with. I struck out every time. Quick. One. Two. Three. Then I went back to the dugout and sat back down. A waste of time.

But, at one game, the coach grabbed me by the shoulders before I got up to the plate. He looked me right in the eye and told me to just imagine that the ball was my "worst enemy." I don't really have a worst enemy, but when the ball flew toward me while I was standing there choked up on my bat, Mr. Nye's tomato-red face appeared on it coming at me fast and before I knew what was happening, I swung the bat with all my might and he went flying over everyone's head. I swear I could hear him scream in pain. I remember my mother's hollering and screaming from behind me. I looked back and she was standing and jumping up and down. I stood there dumb and excited by the fact that I had finally done something to make her happy, until it dawned on me that she was shouting at me to run. I only made it to second base. It wasn't a homerun or anything. But I did score a run and I liked how surprised everyone was. It never happened again, though. So Mr. Nye did help me at baseball once.

He once paddled me for hugging a white girl. Her name was Maria and, one day, after band period, I gave her a hug at the top of the stairs just above his office and she pranced away. When I looked down, Mr. Nye was looking up at me real mad and jabbed his finger toward the floor hard, ordering me to come to him right now. I walked down real slow while he went into his office and came back out with his wooden paddle and he grabbed my arm by the elbow and dragged me outside the school. I didn't say anything. Something told me to be quiet. He didn't say anything either. His face was flushed and his knuckles where white as bone. He took me outside and around the side of the school away from any windows while everyone else was settling into their classes. It was just the two of us and it was cold. He told me to grab my ankles. He was shaking, he was so mad. I turned around and did what he told me to. I grabbed my ankles and looked behind me over my shoulder. I didn't even ask him why he was doing it. I just went stiff like I do at the doctor's office before a shot. All I saw was the paddle swing back high over his head where it hid the sun for a second before I felt the pain. He landed five hard swats to my butt. Each one hurt more than the one before it. Tears came to my eyes but I didn't make much noise. I could hear him behind me breathing harder each time he hit me. His breathing was raspy and heavy, so I could tell that he was using all his strength. When he was done, he told me to stand up and go to class. He wiped spit from his lips with the backside of his hand and looked around to make sure no one saw us. He didn't look at me once. I guess when I hugged Maria, I made her a slut and that made him mad. I didn't know that hugging counted.

I limped to class with my butt hurting and I wondered if I should tell my mother about it and decided not to. She would just yell at me. I had a feeling Mr. Nye wasn't going to tell anybody either, since he took me so far away to do it. This was good because I didn't want to get into any more trouble.

Mr. Nye is at the podium now trying to make a gym full of kids be quiet. He is trying to explain that we students onstage could have a chance to go to a statewide spelling bee in Columbus, our state capital. No one else seems impressed but my hands are shaking. The kids won't settle down so Mr. Nye yells into the microphone, causing it to make a squealing sound and now you can hear a pin drop.

I look into the crowd. There are all white faces on one side and all black faces on the other. But every one of them is wondering what I did to get up here. I look over at Jodie Henderson and she is in her usual pose with her back straight, her hands folded in her lap, and her chin up high. She belongs here. Mr. Nye sits down, and the spelling bee lady calls the first student to the podium to spell first word.

My father wasn't always like he is now. When he worked at Republic Steel, he was always bringing home presents for us, which would make my mother mad because he wasn't saving any money. She was always talking about "saving for a rainy day," but my father wanted us to have fun. One time, he brought home a big round swimming pool and he and my brother set it up in the backyard. It was the only one in the neighborhood and all the kids from the block came over. We had so much fun that day. He and my brother had worked all morning to get the pool set up and by the afternoon, the backyard was full of screaming and splashing. I came up from underwater and I saw my father sitting in his lawn chair smoking a Winston and smiling at all of us. He was wearing his mirrored sunglasses looking proud and happy and throwing inflatable balls into the pool. My mother brought out Kool-Aid popsicles and before we knew it, we were having a backyard party. Too bad it was cut short when somebody peed in the pool and we all had to get out. My mother said that this is what you should expect from Negroes. They don't know how to behave themselves and that some neighborhood kid was probably jealous that we had a pool and they didn't so they peed in ours. Sometimes, my mother sounds like white people. The pool never got refilled after that and eventually it just fell apart in the backyard.

My family doesn't do things together anymore since my father lost his job and started acting weird. We barely speak to each other. The house feels funny to me, like a place I just go to sleep and eat. My mother is always tired from work and my brother and sister and me aren't friends anymore. I'm not sure when this happened, but it feels like there are a lot of secrets in my house. We don't talk to one another and it's like five different people are living five completely separate lives under the same roof. It's every man for himself.

But a long time ago, after my father realized that I wasn't any good at baseball, he came home one day with a giant fish tank. He had bought all the things that it needed like pumps and plants and rocks and even some fish floating in plastic baggies. He called me away from playing jump rope with my sister and told me that we were going to put it all together. My brother even helped us. I wasn't interested in fish, but he made me help. He was smiling and excited. We read the instructions, built up the tank up together and, after a while, I started to like it. It was fun. He was bossy about it, but he was patient with me, and when the time finally came to put the fish in, I was pretty happy with myself.

My favorite was the Siamese fighting fish. It looks like a feather that's come alive. I told my father this and he laughed out loud. You have to lower Siamese fighting fish into the tank inside the plastic baggie separately from the other fish to let them get the feel of the tank and get used to the other fish because Siamese fighting fish are killers. We learned this lesson the hard way when, the next day, there were two dead angelfish ripped to shreds and floating at the top of the tank. We scooped them up with the hand net and my father crossed himself like the Catholics do and made a funny joke about God having to accept the fish in heaven because they were already angels. I laughed but I guess you really had to be there. "We'll get some more fish," he said. "You read about what kinds of fish can live with a Siamese fighting fish and we'll get some more fish." Him asking me to read made me feel like he had actually been paying attention to me and knew what I liked to do. I found out later that the real name for the Siamese fighting fish is *Betta splendens*. Reading is why I can spell words. Reading is the only reason why I am in this spelling bee.

I won't spell words wrong on purpose just so I can go sit down and be done with this. Something won't let me. Even if I tried, I don't think that I could do it because words are supposed to be the way they are and spelling a word wrong on purpose would feel like I was putting my shoes on the wrong feet. So I'm spelling each one they give me the best I can. In fact, I'm feeling a little thrill when

the spelling bee lady says, "That is correct!" after I'm done spelling a word right. Some kids in the crowd clap, but most of them
yawn. Around me, the empty seats onstage are multiplying. They
look like gravestones. I sit up in my chair a little higher each time
a white girl gets a word wrong and has to go back out and sit in the
bleachers. After a bunch of rounds, it's only me and Jodie Henderson and some other girl I don't really know sitting in a graveyard of
misspelled words.

Inside, I am beaming. Maybe I *could* go to the statewide spelling
bee. Jodie Henderson isn't so great. Her mother works at the high
school in the office and that's probably the reason why she's even
here.

I am sitting straight up in my seat now. I put my hands on my lap
the way Jodie Henderson does. I lift my head high and catch Mr.
Nye out of the corner of my eye. The way I'm sitting now makes
him tap another teacher on the shoulder and point at me. They
both laugh. Mr. Nye thinks he is *Betta splendens* and that I am an
angelfish.

Nobody comes to our house anymore because of the way my father
is now. My mother used to have friends over, but now my father
makes them uncomfortable. He says my mother should be focusing
her attention on the family instead of "running the streets." He has
never liked her to have any friends and, since he's home all the time
now, he really doesn't seem to want her to talk to them. He only
has bad things to say. So they don't come over anymore. Instead, he
haunts our house like a ghost.

When he worked at the steel mill, we used to have to go pick
him up from his shift in the middle of the night and, since we only
have one car and my mother didn't want to leave us kids alone in
the house, she would bring us along. In our pajamas, my brother,
sister, and I would pile into the back seat and take our pillows and
blankets with us. It was like a little camping trip, sort of. It only
took like a half an hour, but it was a lot of fun. I used to look for-

ward to it. I liked to press my face against the cool car window and wrap my blanket around me and count the streetlights until we got there. When we did, and my father got into the car, he was like a tornado. He tickled and poked us until we couldn't breathe and he landed big fat kisses on my mother's face until she told him to stop, laughing the whole time. She pretended to be grossed out because he was so dirty from work. But now he just isn't the same person at all. He has said that, when the steel mill closed, they laid off all the Black men first. I think he's still mad about that. Now when he talks, it's only to complain about how terrible every single thing in the world is or to tell my mother that she is ungrateful. When she got a job to help us get off welfare, he was done talking to her for good. It was like she took away the one thing most important to him. He said that my mother wants to act like *she's* the man now. It's like he doesn't even know what to do anymore.

The girl onstage who's not Jodie Henderson just spelled "photogenic" wrong. She missed the second "o." It's an easy mistake to make, but I would not have made it. Now there's only two of us left. I feel like I knew this would happen.

The kids in the crowd are getting more restless. No one cares, but I'm thinking about all the things I'll be able to do with my life when I win. I could become a teacher myself wherever they hire Black man teachers. I will be better than Miss Biviano and treat all my students the same. I won't accuse them of cheating and lying. I won't yell at them all day the way she does. I would be a *good* teacher. I wonder how much money the spelling bee winner for the statewide championship will win. I bet it would be enough to make my father come out of the bedroom. He didn't even get as far in school as I am now and, by winning, I could show him that it might be possible for him to go back and get a new job. It doesn't have to be at the steel mill, even though that's the only job he says he wants. Then my mother could stop working and things would go back to the way they were.

Jodie Henderson and I go back and forth and back and forth and the kids in the crowd aren't even bothering to hide their boredom. But I don't care. I will stay on this stage as long as I have to. The spelling bee lady is calling my name, so I walk up to the podium.

"Brian, your word is . . . 'foreign.'"

"Could you use the word in a sentence, please?"

"The *foreign* dignitaries are meeting for lunch."

"May I have a definition, please?"

I am stalling for time. The word is not appearing in my head like the rest of them do and I know there's a "G" in there somewhere and I know there's an "I" and an "E," but I can't remember in which order they go and now there are seven letters square dancing in my head and I know the kids in the crowd want me to get it wrong so they can leave and I can feel my heartbeat behind my ears so . . .

"Foreign. F-O-R-I-E-G-N. Foreign."

It gets real quiet for a moment.

"I'm sorry. That is incorrect."

I stand with my heartbeat in my ears hoping that I'll be given another chance. "I'm sorry. That is incorrect." I hear it again and I go numb. I turn around slowly and take the longest walk back to my chair, which is getting farther and farther away from me with every step. The crowd is paying attention now. I pass Jodie Henderson who can't wait to get to the podium. She already has a big smile on her face. She is asked to spell the word. She is way too cheerful when she does.

"Foreign! F!O!R!E!I!G!N! Foreign!!"

"That is correct!"

The whole gym explodes with applause. They're loud mostly because of the fact that they get to leave now. But, part of that applause, I know, is because they don't think I deserved to win. I wonder why I am always trying to be something that I'm not. Mr. Nye runs up onto the stage and holds Jodie Henderson's hand like she's some sort of prizefighter. He says some stuff into the microphone as

I sit in my chair never wanting to move again. My shoes are untied. This feels like a practical joke. Black boys weren't meant for schooling and everybody knows that.

On the walk back to Miss Biviano's class, one of the Black boys calls me a faggot and his friends laugh. She hears this and says nothing. I can't be mad at her. Nothing spells "faggot" like being in a spelling bee.

The rest of the day drags on and, when it's finally time to leave, I board the bus and prepare myself to get teased even worse than normal. I lay my head against the window and tell myself that I'll never come back.

My sister is home before I am. When she sees me, she makes a pouty face and tells me that she's sorry I lost and that she was cheering for me. I know that she means that she was doing this silently because my sister never makes a noise. She barely raises her head. She gets teased a lot from boys who tell her she's not pretty and call her "ball-headed" because she cannot grow her hair long and flowy like a white girl. We used to play together. She used to be a lot of fun. We would play dolls and make up dances and I secretly wish she still wanted to do that with me, but I can see that she now has completely different things on her mind. She has become secretive and wants to be by herself all the time in her tiny bedroom.

I don't even want to see my brother when he gets home. He has basketball practice after school and, when he comes into the house grumpy that he has to live here, he'll either make fun of me for making a fool of myself or he will ignore me completely. He doesn't like for me to talk to him in public. I sometimes wish that I could play sports so that I could be a brother he's proud of. He has lots of friends and girlfriends too. They all know my body doesn't move the way his does. He runs track and plays football and basketball and baseball. I am the worst brother for someone like him to have and we both know it. He is so good-looking that my mother doesn't even mind that his Jheri Curl has ruined every pillowcase in the house. The only time we talk to one another is to fight. My parents act like they were forced to live together and now we all act like that toward each other.

My mother isn't home from work yet and my father has made one of his rare trips out into the living room. He sits on the couch in a T-shirt he's been wearing for days. It used to be white, but now the armpits and neck are stained yellow. He is staring at the television set and smoking a Winston. When he sees me, he tries to start up a conversation. I don't know why. He hasn't tried to talk to me in a really long time. He leans forward and puts his elbows on his knees and asks me if I had a good day at school. I don't say anything. I just shrug my shoulders.

He tries again. "Well, what did you do today?"

"Nothing," I say shrugging my shoulders again. "Same as any other day."

There is a commercial for toilet cleaner blaring on the television. We watch it together. As father and son.

Tuan's alphabet song has evolved into a little dance that consists mostly of bouncing and arm flapping. As he sings the first five letters, he flaps his arms wildly and kicks his legs to the delight of not only the cooing woman across from him, but a few more passengers who have noticed him. A newly arrived white woman takes a particular and active interest, as Tuan's father continues on his phone. I am annoyed by her. I want to take the opportunity to tell Tuan to stop dancing in front of this white woman.

She is chuckling at him and waving her fingers the same way the first woman did, but her fawning has caused the hair on the back of my neck to stand on end. I want to get up to block her view and tell Tuan that, when it comes to white people, he has a shockingly short time to be cute before he becomes threatening.

Black boys don't get a long boyhood. It ends where white fear begins, brought on by deepening voices, broadening backs, and coarsening hair in new places beneath our clothing. Then there's our skin, which provides little middle ground. The world seems either fascinated or repulsed by it. Tuan right now is in a perfect place of not knowing any of this. For him, his body is merely a vehicle to run from place to place and explore the world. He is wonderfully oblivious, as I must have been at one point.

Don't dance or sing for them. I hope someone will warn Tuan. Black boys are far more than just their entertainment.

THE RED CABOOSE

Now that I am an adult, I realize that everything I ever learned about white people, I learned from the enormous color television set, a Magnavox, that sat front and center in our tiny, ramshackle living room. It was the only one in the house, and it was on constantly. It served as a clock telling us what time of day it was by whatever show was on. It was a babysitter for when my mother had to go to work and my father laid in bed all day behind a locked door. It was a disciplinarian in absentia when my mother took it away or hung the privilege of watching it over our heads like the Sword of Damocles. Since there was only the one, there were evenings when the fighting over it shut the whole place down. When my mother turned it off as punishment, it sat there, dark and dead of all its potential; drained of all its colors.

It was an almost seaworthy floor model in which a thick glass screen wrapped in a credenza's-worth of lacquered, brown wood was the gateway to all the things in the world that I couldn't have. A crystal ball of covetousness. I sat day after day allowing that television to teach me that the most important thing in life was to be liked. By everybody. Between its teachings at home and social life at school, I learned that the whiter you acted, the better liked you were. So I changed the way that I spoke to mimic the characters on television. I concealed every part of myself that I deemed to be too

"Black." Because my life up until then had shown me that white wasn't just a race, it was a goal. And, at fifteen years old, I decided that this was a goal I wanted to achieve.

Sitting cross-legged and a foot from the screen, I looked up at the TV and learned that white children were ethereally beautiful and perpetually innocent; even their mistakes were charming. White children got sent to their bedrooms or were given a good and loving talking to—punishments that shamed the knee-jerk ass-whuppin's my siblings and I were subject to for a misspoken word or the slightest infraction. I didn't even have a bedroom to get sent to.

White children were given "allowances." Allowances: money that was given to them just for being alive. White children became indignant when their television parents did not raise these allowances or withheld them as punishment for some adorable mistake they'd made. Their household chores seemed more of an option and not a command necessary to keep the very household functioning. Their clothes were never out of style, never dingy with wear. Their homes were beautifully decorated. They all had bicycles and their own bedrooms, and I was in thrall to the opulence and ease of it all. The parents of white children were loving toward each other and playful with their children. They acknowledged them and talked to them and always seemed to be in a good mood.

In contrast, my parents were endlessly angry—either at one another or at their children—and our existence was anything but opulent. Our home was a shack, especially when compared to the two- and three-story palaces that lay just at the other end of town. Money was a constant discussion: lack of it, what to do with it, where it was going to come from. It was always a problem. The white parents on television were always canoodling, doting on their children, and smiling at one another with an air of playful romance, but my mother didn't like my father at all and it was fairly evident. Their utter lack of resemblance to the white parents on television made me wonder why they'd ever married in the first place. They seemed to tolerate each other well enough when my father had a job. But once he lost it, there were chasms of silence between them filled only with duty and avoidance. I didn't quite understand what was going on between them, but they seemed to view my siblings and me as an inconvenience at best. But the white people? They had it all figured out. They always had money. Their problems were fixable within thirty minutes if you added in the commercials for things we couldn't afford. I watched them through the looking glass of the Magnavox with my mouth hanging open, wanting so badly to be a part of their world.

Between the family sitcoms and commercial breaks, there were brief seconds when the screen would go black, and I would see my reflection in the television screen. It was then that I knew I would never get to experience the heady highs of Caucasianism. My skin was so black. I could barely make out my features in the darkness of the glass. I was just eyes looking in on a world that I'd never be invited to join. In those seconds, I wondered if Blackness was responsible for inferiority or if God just made those who were inferior Black.

Growing up, my town was perpetually colorless and damp, even in the summertime, and the place where I showed up every day for education was built like a prison. The school colors were red and gray, like a gunshot wound through an old man's head, and every wall in the high school hallways was painted pea-soup green. There was no place more miserable than my high school. The floors were the gray kind, speckled with different colors like vomit. I would often stare at the flecks, zeroing in on the silver ones and trying to connect the dots. They looked to me like an infinite cosmos, a getaway route I could follow to escape having to use the dreaded welfare lunch card, which glowed fluorescent pink, begging for attention.

When the steel mills in Warren and the Rockwell bumpers plant in nearby Newton Falls closed, every Black family in the area was thrown into turmoil. With no other work options, every Black man in the area was left stunned. Some took to the bottle and became either angry or maudlin drunks. I watched them stumble around the streets of our town and vowed that I would never be so pathetic as to touch alcohol. And because these manufacturing jobs left to seek out greener pastures for their executives, every Black child's hand was holding a fluorescent pink *free lunch* card. I hid mine to avoid the embarrassment. It was a mark, a brand. In the end, it was just easier to skip lunch. I tried to be cool about it even when my stomach growled.

A boy in my class, Alex, embodied all the boys I saw on television. He had a father who wore a suit and tie to work and who would show up for school events and smile at his son lovingly and with open affection like the TV dads. They even hugged. His mother was the typing teacher at the school and surely didn't come home with a scowl carved into her face only to grumble out grievances before she fell into bed exhausted like my mother did. His sister was pretty and outgoing. He had no older brother under whose shadow he lived or was so embarrassed by him that he didn't want anyone to know they were related. I imagined their house to be a three-storied affair—white with brown trim and all manner of shrubbery and flowers surrounding it, which I assume his mother tended to vigilantly in a sun hat with a wide and floppy brim. A house that was a perfect backdrop for after-show credits to roll. Our house was a hovel in comparison.

All in all, Alex and his family were just better people than us. Alex himself was the epitome of the gentle and thoughtful white boys I could only have access to via the electricity running through the Magnavox that my family could barely keep on half the time. He was the exact opposite of the Black boys who gave me hell every day. He was sensitive. I wanted Alex and I wanted to *be* Alex.

Homosexuality, as it so often does, attacked me in my bed in the middle of the night. I resisted with every fiber of my being until I could resist no longer. Alone in my bed, thinking about Alex unendingly, my eyes rolled back in my head, and I didn't quite know what to do with my hands. Much to my shame, I would soon figure that out. I let the thought of him wash over me night after sticky night. I wanted to hold Alex. I wanted Alex, with his chocolate brown eyes and coal black hair, to love me. I didn't even mind his occasional pimples. I thought they were charming. I wanted him to save me and take me away into his television world. I would stare at him openly at school and make a fool of myself by awkwardly trying to talk to someone who was talking to him so I could somehow make my way into his field of vision.

I fought my demons every night and prayed that the Good Lord would take these desires away from me. The Good Lord never did. In fact, He only made them worse. I abandoned all hope. I couldn't stop and decided that hell was where I should end up. But I wanted to take Alex with me.

Onanism became habitual. When I was "done," I would imagine myself in Alex's mother's class and her repeatedly smashing my penis with the manual typewriter on my desk, over and over again, with pure hatred in her eyes for what I'd just done to her son. I had to look this woman in the face every day, knowing that just a few hours before, she had lost her son to me and my wicked imagination. She would come by my desk sometimes to reposition my fingers on the keyboard, and I would seethe with jealousy that she got to see so much of him, but I would also thrill to the thought that maybe she'd recently touched his hair and was using the same hand to correct my hand positioning. I smiled and hoped that she didn't catch a whiff of the lust that might have stubbornly stuck to my recalcitrant fingers despite all of my scrubbing. All of my praying and scrubbing. It was only a matter of time until someone locked me up.

They used to like to watch me dance, the white kids, and I would dance for them. The levels of coonery to which I sank were unfathomable. There were Al Jolson–style minstrel shows given in our high school gymnasium, starring yours truly. A real live Negro. I shucked and jived my way into their hearts every day in the gym after they'd had their lunch. They may as well have thrown watermelon slices as payment. The Black kids from my neighborhood would look on from the other side of the gym, shaking their heads in disapproval. But I didn't care. They were doomed to be Black their whole lives. Plus, they had all called me "faggot" enough to earn my hatred forever. I had found acceptance. That's all I ever wanted. Someone would bring a little cassette deck, and I would dance for all I was worth while they smiled and clapped me on the back and congratulated me for having rhythm. Alex was impressed as well, smiling broadly at me and clapping along goofily to the music. He noticed me in this capacity only and I danced even harder and faster under his gaze until all the others disappeared and I was dancing for him alone. And then, one day, it happened.

"You should *tooootally* come with us to The Red Caboose on Saturday!"

The Red Caboose—Warren, Ohio's hottest dance spot for the high school set for everyone who was anyone. Actually, it wasn't in Warren proper. It was much further away in the super-white neighborhood of Cortland. The invitation to *tooootally* come was squealed out by one of the many white girls with whom I kept company during school hours. They liked when I would tell them how pretty they were, and I made them laugh. I went out of my way to show them that I wasn't a threat.

"Oh my God, I'm soooo serious! You should *totally* come to The Red Caboose on Saturday!"

The rest of the white girls agreed that my dance moves were being wasted in this high school gym and that I would be better served to show them off in public. Even the white boys agreed, and the smile on my face could not have been blown away with dynamite. This was the exclamation that was going to start it all for me. After school, I ran home to ask my mother if she would give me a ride to the club on Saturday night. Her reaction was about what I'd expected.

"You got 'Red Caboose' *money*?"

She complained about gas money. She complained about the five dollars it was going to cost to get into the place. She complained that she would be too tired to pick my ass up at midnight when the club closed. I told her that my father would have given it to me, careful not to raise my voice so much that it completely pushed her over the edge.

"Go ask him, then! See if *he* got it!"

I already knew he didn't.

She shut her eyes tight and balled up her fists in frustration when she reminded me that it was in part due to my father's profligacy that we were in so much debt. I hated him for being useless. But I held my most vehement contempt for my mother because she was the one telling me a million different times, in a million different ways, that we could never afford anything. That people like us didn't do things like this. There was no way for me to impress upon her what a misery my life was, that this was my only chance to break out of the dull, fetid dishwater that was our home life. There was no color between the walls of our home. There was no beauty in my life. It was all pea green, gray, boxed in, and all she could tell me, over and over again, was that we didn't have the money. I hated her. Our whole lives were a Black embarrassment.

My parents didn't even make me a "good" Black. Not honey colored or caramel. They made me the color of a turned-off TV screen and there was absolutely nothing I could do about it. Pitch Black.

I no longer attempted to seek validation from my family. I began to look for it everywhere else. I prayed to God to let me die and be reborn the right way. I didn't care what it took. I would lie, cheat, scheme, and steal to go to The Red Caboose with my friends. I was going to make it happen despite my family. I would find the money. I would find a ride. I was determined to be free. If only for one night, I was going to be somebody else. And the very next week, I had achieved my goals.

The Red Caboose was everything I dreamed it would be: loud music and strobe lights and a sense of camaraderie I'd never felt before in my life. Kids chanted "The roof is on fire!" and the DJ played the latest tunes from Duran Duran and Culture Club. I had gotten there through some fancy footwork wherein I got a ride with one of my white friends who had a brother with a car. I borrowed the five dollars from a white friend as well. The music was loud. The dance floor was in the very middle of the room and it was surrounded by comfy couches with tables and chairs. The lights flashed all around the room in reds and blues and yellows and there was a concession stand that offered the promise of cold pop for those who had exhausted themselves dancing. Most of the crowd was there trying to get to second base, but I had come to dance. Every once in a while, the DJ would shine a spotlight on the best dancer on the floor and I was determined to be inside of it.

When a song came on that I liked, I showed off. I showed off so hard that it was almost obscene. I could finally let loose with my dancing skills and really show everyone how cool I was. I did the Robot, the Running Man, and the Cabbage Patch, and took it from the top all over again. I used my hips and my feet to stake a claim for myself on that dance floor and believe me when I tell you that they noticed. The spotlight followed me like a hungry dog and a circle was made around me on the dance floor more than once. I commanded attention. I held court in the disco-lit corners when the DJ played a song I didn't particularly like. I sat down and crossed my legs and leaned back on the wall with a friend on either side of me telling me how I moved like a rhythmic tornado. I was in my element.

I saw Alex and, oddly, I did not care. He was still beautiful, but he danced badly, and I couldn't risk my reputation being seen with him. His moves were awkward and white boy clunky, and as he danced, he had a goofy smile on his face that I just found untenable. I ignored him. I was asked to dance over and over again, and by the end of the night, I was covered in sweat and friends, and I knew I had arrived. I felt . . . white. I paid no mind to the fact that with every undulation and every song and every request to dance and every utterance of the word *cool,* the night was drawing to a close, and when the lights came on, I was barely aware that I was the only Black person left in the room.

When the last song played by Donna Summer and the club let out, I found myself at a loose end. The friend whose brother had a car was not coming back and I had no money. I had just figured that one of my friends would give me a ride home, perhaps the friend whose brother dropped me off. I waited for her to exit the club, but it was as if someone turned off her enthusiasm for me right when they turned off the music. She seemed nervous when I asked if her dad could give me a ride home. She said, "Sure," but there was something foreboding just behind her eyes. When he pulled up and I went to get in on the rear passenger side of his car, he just looked straight ahead. He looked straight ahead and shook his head no. Wordless. No excuse. Just no. I was not permitted. Not allowed. He wanted no one to see me get into a car with his daughter. When they pulled away leaving me standing there, I was absolutely sure that she was going to be read the riot act for having invited me in the first place.

This scenario repeated itself over and over again in the parking lot that night. I ran from car to car like a fireman collecting donations at a stoplight, and each parent looked straight ahead while their children, my friends, who had loved me just ten minutes before, climbed into the back seats and passenger sides of cars my parents could never afford. The white kids all gave me the same look, which was a combination of *I'm sorry* and *You should have known better.* They all drove away, leaving me alone in the parking lot in the middle of nowhere. I was fifteen, broke, and all out of dance moves. I could see the lights of their vehicles driving off in the distance until they reached the highway, where they just turned into fireflies. I breathed into the cold night air and pressed my tongue to the top of my mouth as hard as I could. I had no idea what to do.

A flier which read "THE RED CABOOSE! TEEN DISCO!" skittered across the pavement in the wind. There was no other word for it, I thought, except "skittered." I liked that word. I said it out loud to myself as I watched the flier scrape across the concrete. It was the only sound I could hear apart from the distant cars on the highway. I watched the wind carry the flier across the parking lot. I looked down at my feet. The very feet that I thought would save me that night, dancing around like a clown. I zipped up my coat until the collar was just below my chin. I don't know how long I stood there silently panicking. I know my fingertips eventually went numb. I had no idea what I was going to do. I was utterly alone.

I don't know exactly when I started to cry. But when I did, it was as if I had been saving it up since birth. There was a river of snot that ran down my lips and seemingly endless tears that I could not turn off and my chest heaved sobs built of pure fear and embarrassment. Mostly embarrassment. I stood there breathing in the cold reality that no one in the world really cared what happened to me.

In a stroke of luck, the refreshment stand man from The Red Caboose came out to throw away a giant sack of trash and I begged him to allow me to use the phone. He grudgingly agreed and when I called my house, no one picked up for several rings, and then my mother's sleepy voice finally answered. She did not ask if I was hurt. The only thing I heard in her voice was deep annoyance and white-hot anger. She swore at me as if she hated my guts. I knew the ride home would be a chilly one; I would just have to endure it.

I sat alone at the entrance of the club under the lit-up Red Caboose sign, waiting. The refreshment stand guy didn't offer to stay with me. When he left, he turned the sign off, walked out the side door, got in his car, and drove away without a word. I wondered if he'd have done that to any of my white friends. I sat in the dark hugging myself against the cold, pulling my collar up over and over again and pushing my wool hat down.

When our enormous hooptie finally clunked into the parking lot an hour and a half later, I could feel the anger coming from my mother before I even got in, which I did without a single word. She was still wearing a headscarf on her head, her pajamas under her bathrobe and her house shoes. And for the first several minutes, we were silent. She kept her eyes on the road, jaw tight. Stewing. But the silence didn't last. She finally let loose with a question that I could not answer.

"What the hell is the matter with you?"

Over the next thirty minutes of driving, my mother told me what a fuck-up I was. She told me how stupidly I'd behaved. She blamed me for my predicament. Apoplectic, she was. She told me that anything could have happened to me out there in the middle of the night. She shouted and seethed all at once. She was angry at having been woken up in the middle of the night to come deal with my stupidity. She would whup my ass if I hadn't gotten so big. Her anger was the only thing holding that car together as it rattled down the highway. She didn't look at me once, but I could see her face contorted in the traffic lights we passed. I felt like she hated me. I felt like a fool.

Her tirade continued unabated. It rose and fell and got silent and then started all over again, from shrieking to mumbling under her breath. It was only when I thought I couldn't take it anymore that we arrived home and she put the car in park. My muscles tensed as I got ready to leap out of the car and rush to my bed to cry some more. But my mother grabbed my wrist firmly and spoke words I will never ever forget.

"Boy, don'tchu *ever* trust white folks again."

I turned and looked out the window in an effort to ignore her words and to stave off shame.

"White people didn't care if you lived or died out there tonight, you understand? Anything cudda happened to you! You gonna get enough of trusting these white people, you hear me?"

I didn't really hear her. I only knew that I had done something wrong in making her get up in the middle of the night. I got out of the car and walked into the house. She, for some reason, remained seated and stayed in the car for a long while before I heard her come inside.

My mother made me pancakes the next day, something that never happened. My parents' apologies always seemed to take the shape of food. Never words. She told me I didn't have to go to church because I'd been out so late. She didn't go either. She told people on the phone what a fool I had been the previous night. They commiserated about white people.

When Monday came, I was armed with new knowledge. It was just the white people in this small town who were the problem. I just had to go to a bigger place is all. Bless my colonized mind, I stood outside the front door of my high school, and I knew what I had to do. I didn't know what internalized racism was and it would take me far too long to learn. The first period bell rang like an alarm clock, and I took my first steps forward knowing only that I had to get far away from this town.

I envy Tuan's father. I admit this to myself as the bus slides into Duquesne, Pennsylvania, a once-thriving place that has been blighted by the loss of the steel industry, just like my hometown.

Tuan's father is young and handsome. Dark-skinned like his son and like me. The boy resembles him so much, one only need to take a cursory glance at the two of them to see the kinship.

I rest my forehead against the cool glass of the bus window like I like to. It shoots my reflection back to me. I look just like my father too. Everyone always says so. Neither of us could be described as good-looking though. Broad, flat noses and sunken eyes that always look bloodshot. There are only two photos of him in existence that I know of. They are of him and my mother on their wedding day. The photo is black-and-white and my mother is wearing a slim white dress and a hat with a tiny veil that just covers her eyes. She is gripping a bouquet of flowers. My father is in a dark suit. My mother's parents, whom I've never met, stand behind the newlyweds in one of the photos and no one looks happy. No one is smiling.

I look past my reflection and take in the bleak sights of Duquesne. It's a poster child for what America does with a town after it's done with it. The sidewalks are virtually empty and the storefronts are boarded up. The town's deadness is made more profound by the knowledge of how alive it used to be. The few people outside walk the deserted and dilapidated thoroughfares in a rudderless, yet agitated way that suggests trouble is about to pop off any minute. This is the way my father walked around our house after losing his job.

He seemed stuck. He had no skills and barely a sixth-grade education. He had only ever worked backbreaking jobs and he believed to his core that this was the only kind of work that a real man should do: hard physical labor.

So he took to complaining. He took to blaming, mostly white people and my mother. She couldn't do anything right. Her dinners all of a sudden became flavorless to him and his shirts were never thoroughly washed. He called her selfish, even though she did everything. Finally she made him leave. And then he became worse. I couldn't stand the sight of him. As I got older, I began to resent the ways in which he seemed to go out of his way to shrink my world. It felt like he was trying to destroy the person I was becoming. I remember the punch I caught to my right temple after I decided that I wanted to dance ballet and he caught me wearing my sister's tights. I remember how he browbeat me when I told my mother that a flower in her garden was "pretty." I wanted to fight back then, but I didn't know how. I was relieved when my mother had had enough of it all and told him to leave.

I like to think she was trying to save me. But I know she was saving herself too.

PARENTAL ALIENATION 101

As part of his daily routine after the divorce, my father stopped by the house to remind my high school–aged sister and an eighth grade me that our mother was an evil woman who was having an affair. My brother was spared my father's visits, having successfully escaped by moving away after graduation.

When my father first began this practice, I dreaded the sound of him banging on the locked back door. He would try to pull it open and my sister and I would look at each other for a moment in a silent game of drawing straws before one of us got up and slowly marched toward it with its doorknob twitching anxiously.

After a while, we stopped locking the door altogether and he didn't even bother to knock. He came to know my mother's work schedule. He learned to look for her car in the driveway. Knowing when she wouldn't be around made him bold. Had my father been able to gain access to the house while we were at school, I'm sure he would have broken in and sat there all day. But he had to wait until my sister and I got home and when we did, the screen door would swing wide and slam, announcing his arrival. He would saunter in without shame and hold my sister and me captive in a classroom of his own making. He would lecture like a college professor, teaching us the ways in which women, especially my mother, were bereft. My sister and I didn't dare say a word in response. Her because she still secretly adored him and me because I knew that one of his punches could fly out of nowhere to connect with the side of my head.

We knew this wasn't his home any longer, and so his daily presence cast a pall of secrecy over the house. I wanted to tell my mother about his visits, but my sister said that we shouldn't. So we didn't.

My father lived alone in a nearby abandoned house just up the road from where he grew up. He had no heat, water, or electricity and he looked like it. His clothes hung from him, grimy and disheveled. He smelled bad. He would visit every day to tell us that the divorce wasn't his fault.

"The role of a woman," he said, "is to obey her man. The woman was only put here by God as a helpmeet for the man."

My sister and I would quietly cast furtive glances toward one another.

I could never watch him raid our refrigerator. I couldn't bring myself to take in the sight of him stealing food from the woman whose character he assassinated, in the home that she had been supporting *by herself* since he lost his job and become a hobo. It was a shoebox of a house that we lived in—one that I hated waking up in and hated being born into. But it was my family's house. It was given to my parents by my mother's father and it was a hideous monument to failure: all plywood and awkward angles with a furnace that never worked, so space heaters were tucked away everywhere, including a large one at the far corner of the room that glowed red and sputtered like a mini-volcano. It made the whole shack smell of kerosene.

There were only two bedrooms for five people, when we were still a whole family. One for my parents and one for my sister. My brother and I slept on the floor and the couch in the living room. I was always the one on the floor. I dreamt only of escaping my house and my town for a real city because I knew a real city was where I would find a bigger world and maybe a little peace. If I didn't make it to New York, maybe I'd try Pittsburgh. I figured they were pretty much the same. I planned to go to college away from home but I knew I'd have to stay in state because it was cheaper that way. That was fine with me. I just needed to get far enough away that nobody knew me or the house that I hated.

I never wanted anyone to see it. I never invited any school friends over and I knew that all the kids in the neighborhood talked about us. They talked about the faux brick façade that was peeling away in sheets and they talked about my father's makeshift "garage" made of paneling and plywood that was just big enough to house the beloved tractor that he also used as a car. It was the house we deserved: a poverty house surrounded by junk and old lawnmower parts that I wanted nothing more than to escape. I dreamed of easy, comfortable living in a pretty home, a home that showed by its very lavishness that my parents loved me.

When I went to school, I pretended that I was from an entirely different family. The lies I told to cover my shame were as extensive as they were ornate. About our "swimming pool," our "housekeeper," my "bedroom." The kind of lies that I would keep telling people all throughout my life. And the more lies I told, the easier it was for me to believe them. I learned to lie about my life with ease. To pretend that I was someone else entirely. I made up stories about my father and mother and how much they adored each other when the truth was that there was no mountain high enough, valley low enough, or river wide enough to compete with the lovelessness of their marriage. But I had found that the distance between who white people already assumed I was and who I wanted to be was only as wide as my imagination. So I learned to lie. Because the only thing I felt when I looked at my family, this house, was shame. And I hated my father. I hated his infectious poverty. I hated his daily visit to pathetically pilfer food and attempt to poison our minds.

"You know ya Mamma ain't at work like she say she is."

Having eaten out of the leftover casserole dish in the fridge, my father moseyed into the living room holding a chicken drumstick.

He never left any evidence of his visits. He was beginning his lecture.

"She out there right now runnin' wit' that nigga in the streets." He gnawed away at the chicken bone.

This was typically how my father started, the way he revved up his engine before the real rant got underway. He would begin with the sins of my mother and then move gradually into the evils of women in general. He would go on at length about how women have forgotten their place in society and how God was displeased with the entirety of their gender. He needed my mother to be weak so that he could feel strong.

My mother had two good friends whose husbands had run out on them and he blamed her friends for poisoning my mother's mind against him. They were jealous, he said, because they were incapable of keeping a man. Then he moved into how all of her friends, at one time or another, had tried to sleep with him.

He sat down on the couch behind my sister and me and set his glass of Kool-Aid on the side table. A glass on which he would leave a greasy fried chicken smudge. My sister and I kept our eyes fixed on the television trying not to absorb his words.

"Shudda never married that damn woman. I was the only one who would help her out. I brought everything into this house and you think I get even a tiny bit 'a consideration? Ungrateful. Runnin' all around town. A woman 'sposed to stay at home and take care 'a the family like it say in the Bible." He sucked loudly on the marrow.

I bit my tongue and leaned closer into the television set. My father was a big fan of God when it served his purposes. He was a big fan of man's dominion over all things. Especially women.

"After them white folks laid me off, she couldn't wait to get out in them streets to find a new man. All she ever did was use me." I heard a chicken bone snap in half behind me.

He would go on like this for hours, taking brief pauses to listen for sounds of tires in the driveway. He had almost been caught a few times by my mother coming home from work early. I relished the possibility. One time, as he was lecturing us, I heard a car pull into the driveway. I prayed it was my mother home early from her job. I jumped up and ran to the door, but it was just a random car pulling into our driveway to turn around and go the other way. When I got back to the living room, my father was gone, leaving my sister standing there looking stunned.

"He jumped out the window."

I looked at her incredulously.

"I'm serious. He ran into my bedroom and jumped out the window."

I didn't believe her. I went to her bedroom and there was her window open wide like an escape hatch, its yellow curtains billowing in the wind. I looked out and caught a glimpse of the back my father rounding the corner, pulling up his baggy pants.

I wanted so much to ask him what he expected my mother to do. He hadn't worked in years, while she took part-time job after part-time job until she found this full-time one. I wanted to ask him if he expected her to just sit at his knee with our welfare voucher in hand and watch him fail. But I knew better. My father's class in parental alienation wasn't open to questions. It was a one-man show. I never challenged him or said anything because I knew that at any moment, his tightly wound tether could snap and that one punch would be enough to silence and punish me for meddling in grown folks' business. We were merely to listen and absorb. So we sat, my sister and I, with our backs to him as my sister dabbed tears from her cheeks with the heels of her hand from listening to his bile.

My mother had already called before he'd arrived to tell my sister and me that she would be late, so I cut up a potato and threw the slices on the stove to make French fries, the only food I knew how to make. My mother made this call often and, if I'm honest, it worked on the suspicions my father had planted in my brain. She was having an affair and that thought didn't bother me as much as the thought that she was out there showing affection to someone that she never seemed to show to me. I pictured her smiling and laughing with this faceless man, happy to be away from all the mistakes she'd left back in this ugly house.

We never told my father that my mother had called to say that she would be late, so he left at his normal time, and my sister and I returned with renewed devotion to the television.

We watched one of our favorite shows. In it, the parents are former hippies who have two daughters and a son. They have a house with an upstairs and all the kids have separate rooms with their own beds. The mother is an architect and I can't remember what the father does. They have "problems" every week because the son is a young conservative and there are minor and hilarious dustups about that. But it is all in good fun and at the end of thirty minutes, they are all in love again each week.

I was fascinated by the family's relationships. I leaned in close to the Magnavox during a scene in which the conservative son is having trouble falling asleep and the mother stays up with him to read him a bedtime story. I was enthralled at how readily white people seemed to openly love one another.

My sister shook me from my thoughts to say that she smelled smoke.

We immediately ran to the space heater, which sat in the corner of the room, going full blast and making the house stink. We were fearful that it had caught the curtains on fire. We shook the curtains but all the space heater did was sputter and belch. No flame had escaped. We ran separately to each bedroom to check the others and, while checking, I remembered the fries that I put on the stove to cook. I remembered how the grease was already hot when I threw them in and how they sizzled. I had been so captivated by the TV that I had forgotten about them. I ran toward the kitchen where the smoke in the hallway became thicker and thicker and I kicked open the back door that my father had walked through only hours before. The smoke blew out in one giant cloud. The whole wall behind the stove was already engulfed in flames.

I heard my sister screaming from what sounded like miles away.

I just stood there. Watching it. It probably wasn't more than a few seconds but it felt like hours. I watched flames lick their way up the wall of all that cheap wood paneling. Electricity ran through me. My breath came faster. My sister's screaming grew louder and more panicked.

I ran for the sink and filled up a pot full of water to aim at the stove and a nagging voice in my head mentioned something about never throwing water on a grease fire but it was too late. The water was already airborne and when it hit the stove, a demonic hiss and sizzle rose up from it and the flames reacted angrily. They grew larger and multiplied. I openly smiled. I wanted to do it again.

One entire side of our tiny kitchen was on fire and the ceiling was following suit. The flames curled and flickered and the blaze was spreading so rapidly that I could hardly believe my eyes.

I think I smiled again.

My sister grabbed me by the arm and pulled me out the door the smoke had just gone through and we stood outside in the cold air, watching, just watching, as the house disappeared into bright reds and yellows. The heat from the flames was soothing on my face. Thick, black smoke rose high from them. My sister's breath came from behind me in short, terrified bursts. Mine remained steady and smooth. I closed my eyes and allowed myself for a moment to hover over the entire scene like a buzzard riding a thermal.

I used to love to play with matches. I would pull one out of the matchbook and light it and then lay it on top of the rest and wait that half a second for when the entire book would flare to make that satisfying "ffftt!" sound. Then they would all be dead. It was thrilling. This is how fast our ugly house seemed to be burning.

My sister and I didn't know what to do, but the house did. It glowed so brightly and the smoke rose so high that the neighbor lady called the fire department. She ran over in her housecoat and was soon followed by all the other neighbors in their housecoats. They gasped and asked questions that I heard none of. I was too busy watching. Too busy relishing.

At one point, a giant hand made entirely of flames rose up from the back of the house, palm and five fingers, to crush it. The house crackled and popped and even though we were all now standing in the road, I could still feel its intense heat. I studied it and imagined how the light must have been playing off my face. The fire had come to save me from poverty. From mothers who were too busy at work. From fathers who dripped verbal poison. From secrets. The fire had come to deliver me to the life I was supposed to be living.

Someone must have told my father about the fire because he arrived and stood far away from me talking to a neighbor. He kept his distance. I couldn't hear him but I felt that he was already blaming my mother for not being at home. When our eyes met, he seemed to be taking in the ruin and loss. He truly had nowhere to go now. I felt powerful. He disappeared into the crowd as it grew larger. The house folded in on itself like it had been punched in the stomach. I felt like a man.

Class dismissed.

When the fire department arrived, white men with hoses and giant rubber boots doused the ruins in water and made the ground muddy. They shouted commands and pushed us away as they scrambled everywhere and lights flashed, but I knew it was too late. I hoped it was too late. I heard one of them say the words "total loss."

My mother arrived. I heard her car door slam before she ran to me and threw her arms around me crying. It was the most love she had ever shown me. The fire was already working.

After all the shouting, there was only smoke and the sounds of mud-sucking boots. Burnt black wood and melted siding. And my mother crying.

My sister and I were placed into the back of my mother's car, where a neighbor threw a blanket over us and we drove off to live with my aunt. I looked back at the smoking husk in the ground and I knew that something better was around the corner. I had read that sometimes fires occur naturally in the forest in order for something greener, newer to grow in its place and as the car pulled away for the penultimate time, I smiled.

That night in bed, I imagined what colors I'd paint my new room in our new house with my new father, in my new family.

The next day, we went to see what we could save. It all looked so much different in the daytime. There was no longer the beauty of living flames to cover up what I had done. Everything was soggy, muddy, and charred; some of it was still smoking. Our family photos were burned beyond recognition. The artifacts of our lives were strewn about and exposed and barely anything was recognizable. My mother broke down in tears again.

Later, neighbor children would ravage the site and read aloud the contents of my sister's charred diary on the school bus, causing her more pain. We lost everything and nothing new had grown. And, instead of erasing our poverty, I learned that I had caused us more. I learned, slowly, that I had destroyed our lives. The church had to take up a collection and living with my mother's sister until we found a new place wasn't easy. She had a life of her own that didn't include children. We stayed with my aunt for a while until my mother was able to afford a small apartment in Warren for just me, her, and my sister.

My sister never spoke of the fire in front of me. Neither my mother nor my father ever asked me what caused it. I'm sure they knew, but they never brought it up to me. They never yelled at me, they never asked me why. Maybe they both felt guilty. Maybe they both just loved me enough never to try to make me feel badly about it.

My sister, mother, and I didn't see my father much after that. Barely at all, really. There was no reason to. When I did see him, he looked more worn, more disheveled, thin as a rake. He would apologize that he had nothing to give me, no money.

"I'd have something for you if them white folks hadn't took my job. I'm just waitin' for them to give me back my job."

They never did.

No one ever rebuilt anything on the plot of land where our house once stood. I went back to my hometown to see it just a short time ago and the only thing still there is the small hill in the yard that once served as home base for games of tag. I stood in the exact spot where my father watched our house burn and where the knowledge that he had no place to come visit his children again must have washed over him. Where he must have known I had stolen that away from him. I stood in the spot where I imagine he realized that everything he believed made him a man had literally gone up in smoke.

I could picture everything where it once was. The front porch where my mother hot-combed my sister's hair. The expansive backyard. The tree that held our swing, now chopped down. The land near the back of the yard where my father had built a grape arbor. The patch where my parents grew a garden so bountiful that it kept us fed all winter from the vegetables my mother took such pride in canning.

I had been so focused on everything I believed we didn't have.

No one has wanted to build on the land where I grew up, although other houses surround it. It remains a strangely barren spot where my shame and hatred took root and have forever sullied the ground.

Tuan is standing again, this time with his head pressed against the window like me. I can see that he is silently thrilled to watch the outside pass in a blur before his eyes. He likes to travel. He likes to be on his way someplace. I can just barely remember first feeling this myself — the urge to go places and see things. But I got in my own way. The closest I ever get now is riding around this city on public transportation.

A lot has happened to me on buses. I have ridden this same route on many occasions long ago in the wee hours, after skulking the gay bars all night long. I would sit in the bars' shadows, downing drink after drink, desperate for some white man to take a liking to me. I have ridden this route at 1:00 a.m. with nurses coming off a late shift, when the homeless are looking to get warm for a little while. I have ridden this same route in the middle of the night when I've felt lonely and didn't have anywhere in particular to go. Just to be moving. I have ridden this same route to watch people board and alight and wonder where they're going and what their lives might be like. There's something calming about this route late at night when it's quiet in the city. There's something soothing about the pale blue, fluorescent streetlights whirling by that makes me feel safe.

One night, a long time ago, I boarded the bus at my usual intersection, which was a few stops up from the old Pegasus club. There was a bus stop right in front of the club itself, but I never wanted anyone to see me standing there. I always walked up a few stops. When the bus came, I boarded it and sat down almost in the exact same spot I'm sitting now. Near the front. I usually liked to sit all the way at the back for maximum envelopment. But that night, there were four men already sitting there. They were drunk from the bar they had just left and behaving in that loud and aggressive way that a lifetime of experience has taught me to steer clear of.

I sat slouched and curled my legs up, placing my knees on the back of the empty seat in front me. I leaned my head on the cool glass of the window just like right now. The traffic light turned green and the bus took off, only to stop right in front of the Pegasus club that I had carefully avoided standing in front of. The bus stopped to pick up Jovan.

I never knew Jovan's full name. He was a fixture at the club. Slim, brown-skinned, graceful, and tall. When Jovan moved toward the dance floor, a path would be cleared for him to wave his arms and kick as high as he wanted, and he would soak up the cheers and applause. He wore makeup. Nothing too dramatic, but always a deep eyeliner and just a whisper of powder blue eyeshadow. His bracelets and chains announced his arrival even inside the loud club, and he wore his hair in a Marcel wave. Fried, dyed, and laid to the side.

Jovan boarded the bus as languid and graceful as a princess boarding a horse-drawn carriage. Our eyes met briefly. He knew me from the shadow-hiding I did at the club, but nothing beyond that.

The roughhousing and boisterousness from the men behind me went completely and deathly quiet. I slumped down further in my seat. I could smell Jovan's floral perfume as he breezed past. I don't know where he sat. The scene plays out predictably.

"Would you look at this shit?!"

The men behind me are laughing uproariously. I feel my

shoulders raise up toward my ears. I am practically fetal in my seat, with my knees to my chin. Not because I'm worried for Jovan but because I'm afraid he will look to me for help.

"Nigga, is you a man or a woman?"

My eyes are straight ahead locked on the seat back in front of me, but I can feel Jovan bristle. The energy of the bus has changed. Jovan's voice is nasal, high-pitched, and feminine.

"I'm more man than you'll ever be and more woman than you'll ever have."

This is a response I'd heard before from drag queens, but its cleverness is lost on the men at the back. They lay into him verbally. They tell him that his mother didn't raise him right. They tell him that he needs to be ashamed of himself. That he's going to hell.

They continue. "You need to go home and wipe all that shit off yo' face."

"And you need to leave me the fuck alone."

There is something about Jovan's tone that the men don't like. They don't like how confident he is. They think that he should be the weak one and they should be the strong ones. I hear them stand. I hear them approach him. I'm trying to pretend that I don't notice what's happening behind me as they begin what I can only assume is a campaign of physical harassment. I am too afraid to look back. All I hear are smacking sounds and Jovan screaming "Quit it!" over and over again. He yells for the driver.

"Driveeeeer!"

And the bus stops.

But the driver does not admonish the men. He only looks up annoyed in the bus's rearview mirror and offers to let Jovan off to wait for the next bus. I hear Jovan push past the men and rush past me to the front.

He turns to leave and points his finger back toward the inside of the bus. He glares at the men.

"Fuck you! Fuck you! Fuck you! Fuck you!" And one for the driver. "Fuck you!"

They all laugh.

Then he turns to me but not with his whole body. Just his eyes. He narrows them hatefully.

"AND FUCK YOU!"

He storms down the steps of the bus and back onto the street.

I told myself then that if Jovan didn't want to be harassed, then he shouldn't have gone out looking like that. I remembered the childhood lessons I received from my father and my friend Corey. There is no crime greater than a Black man acting like a girl.

Recently, I've seen Black boys on this same bus huddled up together, holding hands and whispering sweet nothings. They are unapologetic — stronger, prouder, and braver than I was. Than I am. Than I ever have been.

THE RENT

I knew that if I stayed in Warren, I would wither and die. It was my worst fear. So I told my family that I was going to college. My parents couldn't afford it, so I got as far away as I could afford, which was exactly 44.3 miles. I went to the University of Akron with my eyes wide and my heart open. I enjoyed my classes and met a few people that I liked. The only downside was my living situation.

During my fourth week of collegiate freedom, I returned to the house that I shared with four baseball players to find them all in the living room area. I had classes all day and was lucky enough to have landed a nearby cashier job at a twenty-four-hour gas station and mini-mart at night. I was still wearing my humiliating smock when I returned to the house. It was a rarity to see all my roommates in the same room together. They were usually scattered about the messy house: one draped over the couch staring dumbly at the television, another locked in his room with a giggly girl, the third drinking beer and playing cards in the basement with his friends, and, finally, there was Larry, who was perpetually behind the bathroom door on the toilet, grunting.

As I entered, I said hello in passing as I always did. They said nothing. This was also typical, and it suited me just fine. I didn't break stride as I headed up the stairs. They had already established in their minds that I was an oddity. I was unable to banter with them or discuss anything in which they held interest. My jokes were met with blank stares and I generally made them all uncomfortable. But it was the only place I could afford because I had waited until the last minute to secure housing. I'd found their ad in the student newspaper and had taken the room immediately. I decided that this situation was the price I had to pay for not knowing what I was doing. For being too slow. I'd do better next year. I just had to stick it out and endure my roommate situation—for which I was terribly mismatched—for one school year.

I made it to the top of the stairs.

"Brian, we wanna talk to you."

This was unprecedented. They were always monosyllabic and standoffish, and I couldn't imagine what they'd have to talk to me about. I could feel them avoiding me at all times in the house. I had heard them through the walls at night telling their girlfriends how weird they thought I was. When I was around them, I always tried to comport myself in a manly way. I kept my voice at a respectable baritone at all times. I monitored my walk, making sure that it was stiff and straight-backed. Respectable-like. I answered them with the appropriate three-word maximum masculine retorts, and I was flawlessly evasive when asked about "pussy." I was so careful. I kept to myself. I stayed in my room. But I guess it wasn't working.

I ignored the inside jokes they shared at my expense that were so transparent that I sometimes filled in the punch lines for them. Whenever they *did* talk to me, I rarely understood a word they said through the wads of chaw always shoved between their bottom lips and gums. Chaw that ended up spat into empty beer cans and glass tumblers littered throughout the house. I turned to face them.

"Talk to me about what?"

"Can you come down here? We just have some house stuff we wanna talk about."

I descended the stairs, eyeing them with concern and curiosity. They couldn't possibly pin any mess around the house on me. I always stayed in my room and I never complained about the cans of viscous, brown spit everywhere. I never complained about the liquor bottles and mountains of takeout containers. Their loud parties that made me a prisoner in my own room. One night, when they thought I was asleep, two of their drunken party friends crept into my room. Two white girls who tippy-toed in for what reason, I did not know. I just laid there in the dark as they crept toward my bed. I didn't say anything because I was afraid. I was always afraid. I always avoided conflict no matter what. So, they tiptoed toward my bed and lifted the sheet a little on my naked body.

"See? He *is* black all over!"

Then they ran out.

I couldn't imagine what my roommates wanted to talk to me about. I knew that my rent check had cleared, so it couldn't be that. None of them looked at me. Larry, the toilet grunter, sat hunched over with his elbows on his knees and his massive head in his hands, his chin nearly touching his chest to avoid my eyes. When I reached the bottom step, I sat on it. There was a dry, clock-ticking silence for a while which I broke by asking "What's up?" trying to sound casual while they all looked back and forth to one another. It was finally Sam, the clean-cut one, who spoke first.

"Look, man. We know you're gay and we just don't want you bringin' any of that shit into the house."

A plate glass window shattered inside my chest.

"We know, alright. So, we just want *you* to know that we don't care as long as you don't bring that shit into this house. We live here too."

"I want him to move out." Larry the Toilet Grunter didn't look at me and spoke only to the other men in the room. "I want him to move out right fuckin' now. This is bullshit! Tell him to get his shit. He shudda told us up front!"

Had I not been sitting, I would have fallen to the floor. The room tilted. My extremities belonged to someone else. Fingers, toes, all gone. The denials came, fighting their way to the surface for air like passengers thrown overboard.

"What are you talking about?"

My voice shook despite my best efforts. What was meant to sound indignant came through only as a whisper. The words fell out flat and atonal, sounding nothing remotely like a question.

"See! I knew he was gonna fuckin' deny it!" Larry turned to face to me directly and I was sorry he did. His face was contorted to an apoplectic crimson. He pointed his finger. "We *know*, okay? They act like they don't care," he gestured toward the others. "But I do!" I'm not gonna live like this and I don't want that shit *around me* at all!"

The two other roommates, who were so indistinguishable from one another that they blended into one person to me, had remained silent up until this point. Now they mumbled their agreement with Larry. They all began to argue with one another as though I wasn't there, and I sat on the bottom step as their voices became the sound of static and barking dogs. I had been so careful and yet here I sat, undone. Clean-Cut Sam spoke again.

"Look, Brian. We just know and we don't want it in the house. We suspected it and now we know. We don't even care as long as you pay the rent. But just so you know, we don't want it around us."

I didn't know what he meant by *it*. What did that mean? What was I not supposed to do? I wished he'd be more specific so that I could figure out what I had done wrong. How had I given myself away? He went on. "We don't want you making any kind of a big deal about it around us. Cool? Are we cool?"

I spat up a few more denials. They landed like dead birds falling from the sky. I tried my best to make my face look incredulous, out-raged, and offended. But I could tell by their stony eyes that my face was betraying me, just as the rest of my body had throughout my life. I wanted it to be straight and it wouldn't. I wanted it to be good at sports and it wouldn't. No matter what I wanted in life, my body was always there to oppose me. And now here it was again, making a fool out of me. In the end, I feigned exasperation and stomped up the stairs, leaving them talking about me in hushed tones.

When I got to my room, I sat at my desk under a thin layer of sweat and the usual deep shame. I stared at the wall for a long time. Numb and frantic. On the desk was a flier I had gotten from the University of Akron Gay and Lesbian Task Force. I had screwed up all my courage a couple of nights before and attended my first meeting. I had met some nice people and was looking forward to attending another. I had even found myself a nice "boyfriend" and he and I had fooled around a little.

The flier sat slightly askew from where I knew I'd carelessly left it. I picked it up slowly and stood up to slide it into my pocket, as though this act would magically erase the last ten minutes. It didn't work. I heard one of my roommates laughing downstairs and my heart began to race. I had ruined my entire life because of a flier, a bit of paper that promised hope.

I've always had a weakness for fliers. It was a flier hung up at my high school that had led me to this university in the first place. I tore it off a corkboard in the hallway and shoved it into my pocket. In seventh grade, I'd brought home a flier advertising ballet lessons for boys and my father looked at it in disgust, tore it in half, and screamed at me about being "sissified." He shook my shoulders violently in an attempt to dislodge what he believed to be the girl in me. He seemed to believe that if he just shook hard enough, maybe he could make me sick enough to vomit the sissy up onto the floor where we would both stare at it and laugh together before he made my mother mop it up. I sat back down at my desk and removed the Gay and Lesbian Task Force flier from my pocket and cursed it. I ripped it just like my father did and then asked both halves what in the world I was supposed to do now.

I had run from my hometown to Akron with the hope of finding friends and acceptance. I found a few friends in my short time there. But they weren't enough to fill the void I felt. I would have to run yet again to discover some semblance of what I was looking for. Because that's what I did then. I ran.

Pittsburgh, 1992

My first gay pride parade was in Pittsburgh, Pennsylvania, in 1992.
I went, not because I was proud to be gay. In fact, the opposite was
true: I was still deeply ashamed.

I went because I was lonely and horny, because I wanted to find
a new boyfriend. It rained all day. The whole city was one muddy,
gray pigpen and the rain couldn't make up its mind between being
a torrential downpour and a slow, miserable dribble. I wore flannel
because I had been to a few gay bars at that point and noticed that
all the boys wore flannel shirts with the sleeves cut off. Flannel was
really big in the early nineties. My combat boots sunk deep into the
mud with each step and I was trying for all I was worth not to look
terrified.

By the time I arrived in the area of Schenley Park called the Fruit
Loop, I was sopping wet. The Fruit Loop was a stretch of road on
Prospect Drive, the end of which loops around in a circle. It was
where gay people, mostly men, would hang out, sunning themselves
in the summer. These dual details gave the area its nickname. I had
heard tell of other, more lascivious activities that went on in the surrounding wooded areas as well, but this day it was to be the site of
activism.

I learned about the gathering from a flier, courtesy of group
called BiGALA, a new organization at the University of Pittsburgh.
I snatched the flier off a light pole and shoved it into my pocket. I
was determined to go through with this. I had been in the city a few
years and had only visited gay bars to stand in the shadows alone. I
never talked to anyone.

By the time I arrived at the Fruit Loop on the day of the march,
it was a mud pit and those gathered weren't in the best of spir-
its. It wasn't dark like Pegasus or The Holiday, the only two bars
that I had been to. I had only seen other gay people under cover of
night, and it began to me to feel like where we belonged. Where we

should stay. I wondered how these people here out in the bare sunlight could be so devoid of the shame that was creeping its way up my spine. There weren't enough people in attendance to hide me. Everyone seemed to know one another. I stood under a tree on the periphery, trying to strike poses that made me look like I might be a part of things. People smiled at me weakly from time to time but didn't seem to want to approach.

Everyone was busy fighting the rain and the mud, covering one another with umbrellas while they readied their homemade signs. There was a small group of lesbians carrying bongos around their necks and a few cars displaying signs that read GAY RIGHTS NOW and QUEER AND PROUD. I decided that this was all too much and a familiar dread filled me. Heart racing, I searched frantically for a direction to run.

Akron, 1988

I waited in my room for my roommates to all go to their bedrooms. I sat on the edge of my bed with my breath coming in shallow bursts and fighting back tears. I flinched at every loud noise, fearing that, at any moment, Larry would burst through my door to throttle me. I heard my roommates' doors close one by one. I quickly grabbed up a random assortment of underwear from drawers and papers from surfaces, not knowing or caring what I was throwing into a bag. I snatched clothes from the closet so fast the hangers were left swinging and naked on the rods. I raked my cassette tapes off the shelf and into the bag and bid farewell to the room I had known for such a short time. I said my goodbyes to it and to higher education. I said goodbye to Grace Jones, whose *Nightclubbing* poster I'd only installed on the wall with Scotch tape a few days before. She stared at me as I stood there giving the room a final once-over. Her cigarette was tucked neatly into the corner of her full, gorgeous lips. Her stare laid my cowardice bare and her eyes followed me for the whole time I slowly closed the door. And when I did, when the latch clicked, I heard the Scotch tape give way from the wall, rendering her limp. I heard the poster tumble to the floor.

I ran to the mini-mart where I worked. My coworker Denise looked up from her magazine as the bell above the door chimed.

"Damn, boy, whass wrong? You look like somebody just died. Did somebody jus' die?"

"Can I use the phone, please?"

It was 2:00 a.m., and the mini-mart was deserted. There was just me and Denise. I liked her. She wasn't a student. She was a mother with three children and a husband at home, which made her old to me. She wore cornrows that went sideways across her head and she chewed gum all the time. She popped it frequently by inhaling and using it to punctuate her words. She never asked me about girls or sports. Together, on the night shift, she opened magazines and showed me pictures of her favorite male celebrities: Denzel Washington and Eddie Murphy. "Ooooh, ain't he fine?" she would say holding the up picture in front of my face. "I guess," I would answer, shrugging my shoulders and knowing full well that I wholeheartedly agreed. She would just smile and look at me in a way that suggested that I would tell her the truth in my own due time.

I asked her again. "Can I please use the phone?" She reached under the counter and stared at me suspiciously as she handed me the phone.

I called the only person I knew to call in times of crisis. Denise pretended not to listen, but I know she heard every one of my pleas. After I hung up, I couldn't stand her eyes on me, full of concern and questions. I told her that I'd just had a fight with my roommates. It was as close to the truth as I could get. She told me not to worry. She told me that we'd all be made up by tomorrow. She'd seen this kind of thing before with students.

I went out and sat on the curb just in front of the store beside the ice machine. She came out occasionally to check on me. She gave me a Mountain Dew. "Mountain Dew is for white folks," she said, "but I drink it when nobody here."

In that moment, she created within me the odd sensation of laughing through a deep ache. Like remembering something funny someone you loved once said while you're sitting at their funeral. The feeling that confuses your body in an exhilarating way and you can't differentiate between the tears born of mirth and the ones born of sorrow. Joy and pain get all mixed together in a yarn ball of emotions.

I cried so much that I believe Denise knew that this was about more than just a mere fight with roommates. She sat with me on the curb and cemented her place as one of the first in the mosaic of Black women who have saved my life. When a customer came, she went back inside. But right after, she would come out to sit with me. We talked about all sorts of things. Sometimes we just sat there silently. She went back inside one last time before I saw the familiar headlights of the vehicle that had carried me to this place weeks beforehand. My mother in our ratty, old Buick had come to save me. When she pulled up, I threw my bag in the back and climbed in. She was wordless and angry. The kind of anger that comes from having been woken up in the middle of the night by your hysterical son and driving an hour only to find that said son is still in one piece. As we drove away from the rubber capital of the world for the last, last time, Denise emerged from the mini-mart in the rearview mirror. She waved goodbye high over her head and I waved back weakly when I was sure that she was far enough away that she couldn't see me. Besides running, hiding was the only other way that I knew how to deal with a bad situation.

Pittsburgh, 1992

I was hiding behind a tree at Pride when Annette found me.

"Would you like a sign to carry?"

The rain was falling so hard that she had to yell. I heard her clearly but asked her to repeat herself just to buy some time. "Would you like a sign to carry?" she asked, louder. "We've got extras!" She was smiling at me. One of the lesbians with the bongos. She was the only other Black person that I'd seen there. Her almost perfectly round face was accentuated by her completely shaven, bald head. She had kind eyes and was struggling with her umbrella and a few poster board signs that had gotten wet. We shouted over the sound of rain battering the tree over our heads.

"I'm really not sure I'm gonna go at this point!" I shouted.

"Oh, but it's gonna be so much fun!"

"I don't have any way to get to the . . ."

"We'll give you a ride! I'm Annette!"

She thrust out her hand and I told her my name. She handed me a sign and I took it. I don't know why. She told me to follow her. She was authoritative and direct. As we trudged through the mud to her ride, she told me that she was a member of BiGALA at the university and that they were looking for more people to join. Particularly people of color. She was glad she ran into me, she said. She talked endlessly about how much this march meant to her and how much we were going to shake things up. I was only listening to the voice in my head telling me to escape while I could. But I followed her because I was afraid not to. I followed her because I felt that, if I didn't, I would be lost forever. I followed her because she was, up until that point, the bravest person that I had ever met, and I was ashamed to be as afraid as I was in front of her.

We arrived at an old van which several other people were loading up. She introduced me around quickly and we all piled in. The only seats were in the front, so most of us sat on the floor in the back, unsecured by seat belts. We jostled with the movement of the vehicle and the ride was damp and silent. People made nervous chitchat from time to time, but I could tell that these people were all just as afraid and nervous as I was. The van hit bumps and rattled all the way to downtown Pittsburgh and we sat there, shoulder to shoulder, wondering what to expect next.

Akron, 1988

For most of the ride from Akron back to Warren, my mother and I drove in tense silence, both of us with our eyes fixed unflinchingly on the road. She had come to save me in the middle of the night again. She was still wearing her slippers and looked tired.

I had made such a big deal out of going off to college. Bragged about it. My mother didn't understand why I was going, and she frequently asked me why I just didn't go into the military. She didn't have the money to pay for school and told me so many times. But I worked at Kmart, convinced her to get a loan for me, and secured enough funding to go.

Now she was picking me up from school in the middle of the night.

She did not ask me what happened to make me call her, begging to be rescued. But I could see the questions just behind her lips, banging against her teeth from the inside. I put my head down and stared at my lap not daring to cast one look in her direction for the entire ride. When we arrived back home in Warren, I went straight up to my room and I stayed there. I grew roots into the bed while I stared up at the ceiling and allowed a deep depression to erode my bones.

I spent weeks on end withering away. Just the thing I had fled Warren to avoid.

I hoped to rot.

My mother got over her anger after a while and brought food up to me and, when I wouldn't eat, she became worried and turned to Jesus. She came to my room and prayed over me just like the time when I was a child and I got a nosebleed that wouldn't stop. She bent me over the bathtub while blood gushed from my nose and she prayed so hard that she dammed up the river.

My mother never asked me what was wrong or what happened. If she had, I would have lied. Part of me believes that she really didn't want to know. My family didn't talk about things like this. The expression of feelings was discouraged. Dismissed as sentimental foolishness. It was part of our unspoken code. We didn't have the language for it. All my mother knew was that something was desperately wrong, that I was sad. And that seemed to be enough information for her. She never asked if I wanted to go back to Akron to retrieve the rest of my things. She knew better. The house was electric with a secret that no one wanted to discuss.

She came to my room in the middle of the night and sang "This Little Light of Mine," in an effort to cheer me up. I repaid her by drinking bleach the next day, in an effort to put my light out forever. I heard her pacing the floor just outside my door at times.

After several weeks, my mother sat at the edge of my bed one night at her wit's end and told me that I needed to do something. That I needed to get out of that room. I didn't want to cause her any more distress by haunting her house like my father had. I didn't want to be the burden. I didn't want to bring the shame of what I was on her. I looked up from my pillow and, in a voice that I hadn't used in weeks, told her that I wanted to move to a new place. A brand-new place. The place I had once visited on a marching band trip a long time ago.

Months later, she drove me to Pittsburgh and, when I saw the skyline from a distance, I had hopes that I would somehow get lost somewhere within it.

The skyline of a city looks different when you approach it with hope as opposed to approaching it with terror. I was optimistic. I fantasized that maybe I would find a man who liked me, and we would live in a little house together where no one had to know what we were. We would keep to ourselves and adopt a dog. Above all, we would be discreet about our relationship and live quiet lives. Because we would both know that, although we loved each other, there was absolutely no need to make a big spectacle of ourselves. We would never march in any Pride parade.

Pittsburgh, 1992

In the van headed to the Pride parade with Annette and her friends, the buildings of downtown Pittsburgh got larger and larger the closer we got to them. The rain changed its mind again and faded to a drizzle. More marchers had arrived from other places, but there still weren't many. We were sparse. We were all young, mostly in our twenties, carrying homemade signs, and wet and grimy. There were no giant flags, rainbows, or balloons. Our parade was made of flannel and mud, drab and monochrome. The women led the charge, chanting slogans and banging bongos. Fists were airborne and voices were raised. We were marching from the Civic Arena down to the center of town known as The Point to hold a rally by an enormous fountain. I looked down to realize that I had forgotten my sign by the van and, therefore, couldn't use it to cover my face. The street had been reluctantly blocked off by the city to allow us sinners to shout into a void.

There were no supporters on the sidelines. No people cheering us on. There was only the usual downtown Saturday foot traffic of people doing Saturday things. A smattering of people sneering and, even worse, laughing at us. Straight, Black boys pointed—doubled over with laughter like the ones back at school when I would walk down the hall. In a moment of bravery, I turned my head slightly just in time to see a woman mere feet from me retrieve her Bible from her purse and wave it at me angrily. She looked like my mother. We were curiosities to most and a bane to the rest.

I was not brave that day. I walked just at the outskirts of the parade proper, to look like I wasn't really involved. One of Annette's male friends grabbed my hand and held it. I wanted more than anything to wrench it from his grip but I didn't. I was afraid to offend him. Always afraid. I was not proud that day. I was anathema to what that pitiful little parade was supposed to be about. I was scared, and not just of the people on the sidelines and what they thought of me. I was afraid that this was the beginning of a whole new world. I turned my head again to take in the shouting clan with whom I had just associated myself. Their resolve was complete and fearless. Something had kicked in with them that hadn't with me. They were determined. Shouting at the world.

I felt a bit stronger in the knowledge that I wasn't completely alone. But I knew I still didn't belong. There were so many white people. Pride is for white people. But then I looked over at Annette in mid bongo-strike. So much confidence and strength contained within her petite, Black body. She looked up at me and winked. She was wearing denim overalls with no shirt underneath. Defiant.

My mother, Denise, Annette.

When I was a kid, I thought that the key to being a Black man was to learn how to properly lean on things to look cool. What I didn't know at the time is that what Black men lean on the most, whether we want to admit it or not, is Black women.

People marched with linked arms that day in Pittsburgh, to the beat of Annette's bongos. I allowed myself to disappear into her noise and whisper the chant quietly to myself.

we're here. we're queer. get used to it.

I didn't dare shout. No one could hear me but me as I, just under my breath, announced my arrival on the scene.

The relative quiet of the bus is disrupted by the people who board on Duquesne Avenue. Three Black men and three Black women. They laugh loudly and poke at one another in such a way that I can tell they are couples. Displaying their affections openly. Bodies relaxed.

Each of them waves their pass over the fare sensor, making a pleasant "DING" sound. I notice a sign next to the driver reminding me not to harass or molest him under penalty of law. He gives the group a deep nod and closes the door behind them.

As the couples make their way through the aisle, they all stop to say warm hellos to Tuan and his father. The men engage in elaborate handshakes and the women place their hands on their knees to bend over at the boy.

"Hiiiii Tuaaaaaaaan!"

Tuan covers his face but I can see his smile peeking out.

As they near my row, I instinctively grab my oversized suitcase from the floor and place it on the seat next to me. It doesn't matter. They are paying me no mind whatsoever and giggle, joke, and flirt their way to the back where I'm sure, if I turned around, I would see them sitting atop one another, gazing into each other's eyes.

I look over at my suitcase, at this barrier that I've put up. It's a good suitcase. Sturdy and brand-new. I saved for it. But, no matter how well-made it is, no matter how sturdy and new, no matter where it signifies I'm going or where I've come from, my suitcase will not prevent me from being called a faggot. Yet I've placed it here between myself and the Black heterosexuals for good measure.

Growing up, it didn't take me long to learn that my gayness detracted from my Blackness. Black, gay men are punch lines to the Black community. An anomaly to be ridiculed. Relegated to the role of church choir directors. We are a nationwide family secret, courtesy of masculinity and religion.

I stare at my suitcase on the seat next to me and think about why I am often afraid of my own people. Afraid all the time that I'm not "Black enough." Not Black enough because I am not man enough. Not man enough because I like men.

What do you do when your own people don't want you? How do you become anything?

When I was a boy, I used to fantasize that, one day, a big spaceship would come and take away all the Black people to a faraway Eden. The spaceship would loom large in the sky and wait for all of us to get on. As I got older and realized who I was, I stopped having this fantasy. I knew that my own people would never allow me to board.

The telephone of Tuan's father rings again. He looks at the screen annoyed, rolls his eyes, and throws his head back, making a big show of how irritated he is before he pushes a button to decline the call. When he does, it rings again immediately. He declines it. It rings again. This plays out two or three more times before he finally answers it, ready to brawl.

"Hello?!"

The disembodied voice of Tuan's mother comes through loud and clear on speakerphone. The first words she says are "Mutha fukka." This, for some reason, makes me smile. I decide that I like her. Tuan's father takes the phone off speaker quickly, puts the phone up to his ear, and turns away. He places a finger in the other ear like famous singers do sometimes. He is listening to everything he's done wrong this week and has been reduced to stammering, occasionally punctuated by a childish "Awwwww, maaaaan!"

Meanwhile, the bus is gradually getting fuller. The three couples at the back of the bus are audibly falling in love. I can hear them cooing and laughing. I pretend to stretch, raising my hand up high so that I can look back and observe these chirping birds. I rest one arm around my suitcase as if I'm putting the moves on a movie date.

One woman has thrown her legs over those of her boyfriend and is pecking away at her phone. The next is resting her head on her boyfriend's chest as they take a selfie, and the third couple is just outright kissing.

I turn my attention back to Tuan's father and it appears that he and the woman on the phone are making up. Just that quickly. He is smiling and laughing at whatever she is saying. The bus is sailing on a sea of Black love and not a drop for me to drink. I feel jealousy wash over me. People will tell you that times are different now, but I think we all know that only some love is granted public access. It's not as though I want to display affection publicly. It's just that I'd like to have the option.

I snuggle up close to my suitcase and think about all the times I wandered in the dark trying to find somebody to love me. Or at least to take me for the night.

WE LURK LATE

ARENA

The only two things in life that can tell you who you really are—what you're really made of—are war and public sex. I know nothing of war except the images I've seen of desperate men locked in combat or wandering around the battlefield, exposed and vulnerable. I know perhaps too much about public sex.

When I say "public," I am not referring to that vanilla, elevator sex that men and women have in psychological thriller movies: the muscle-stud with perfect hair who grabs hungrily at some sexy inge-nue's panties in an area where they may or may not get caught, like a coat check room or the back of a limousine. Straight people think they're so adventurous.

No, I'm talking about full-on, ass-out, naked body contact with strangers that you've only caught glimpses of in the dark. I'm talk-ing about insertions. Wet moments. The kind of furtive and dirty coupling where it would be rude to stop in the middle just because you've discovered that your partner is missing a limb. I'm talking about the kind of adventurous sex that gets men killed.

I'm talking about gay bath house sex.

The kind we used to have in the mid-nineties before gay men be-came s'damn cuddly. I'm talking about Arena Health Club in Pitts-burgh, Pennsylvania, sex. A place where filthy, public sex was not only encouraged, but mandatory. If you walked inside the Arena

Health Club, you better have been ready to fuck. Pick someone. Anyone. If you weren't engaged in the act of coitus at the Arena, you would be asked to leave. No questions asked or answered.

My first time at the Arena was due to too many drinks, my first blast of cocaine, and my big mouth. The cocaine was incredible, and I tried it mostly because I wanted my new friends to like me. I pretended as if I'd had it thousands of times, when truthfully I had only learned how it's done moments before when I watched them fish dollar bills from their pockets, roll them up, shove them up their noses and deeply inhale lines from the back of the toilet seat in the men's room stall at the club. They tilted their heads back covering one nostril and then made sounds as if they'd just been splashed in the face with cold water. I mimicked them, trying to make a big show of how savvy I was. I rolled up my bill, shoved it up my nose, leaned over the toilet seat, and promptly exhaled, blowing cocaine in all directions. My companions sighed deep sighs and laid out another line. I tried again. And when that line hit my system, I knew immediately that cocaine would be a mainstay in my life. It made me feel invincible. In an instant, I was the person that I always wanted to be. It hit my nasal passages and burned so much that I fanned my hand in front of my face like I had just eaten a ghost pepper. But after a few seconds, the drug worked its way to the back of my throat, filling it with that new car smell. Dark corners of my brain that had lain dormant for my entire existence suddenly lit up and sprang to life. My eyes widened and my shoulders relaxed.

I had been hanging out at the bars with two friends, Tate and Jeremy—both bona fide sluts—and after a long and unsuccessful evening of trying to get laid, they suggested that we go to the Arena. I did not know what the Arena was. I was still new to the scene but wanted to seem experienced.

The blow they'd offered to me hours before was still working its magic. It forced words that weren't true to escape the lips that I

couldn't seem to stop chewing on. Eventually, the drug took control
of my entire mouth. The words felt so good and free as they flew
from between my teeth and tongue, endless and meaningless, until
eventually my words told them that, sure, I had been to the Arena
a thousand times before. My words told all of us that I knew the
doorman and the doorman knew me and that, at the Arena, we'd be
welcomed with open arms. Between frequent and jerky drags of my
cigarette, I told them to stick with me because I knew the Arena
like I knew the palm of my hand.

These were the heady days of gay sex positivity. After the onslaught of AIDS, we were all trying to reclaim our sexuality in bold,
daring, and unapologetic ways. I was just trying to claim mine for
the first time. But I pretended that I'd had a lot of sex. All kinds.
Whips. Chains. Top. Bottom. Autoerotic asphyxia. According to my
words, I had done it all. But the reality was that I had never had sex
beyond occasional romantic interludes when I was only eighteen
with one long-gone boyfriend who had been as clueless as I was. We
didn't know what we were doing. We were gentle with each other.
He asked if he was hurting me and asked if I was comfortable and
smiled down at me. Sometimes we just gave up in the middle and
watched old movies instead.

But Tate and Jeremy had a handle on this sex thing. They had
gripped it by the shaft and milked it for all it was worth. They were
my idols, both twenty-two years old, the same age as me, and were
so much more grown-up and casual about this gay thing. They
pulled it off flawlessly. They were aloof and bitchy. Stylish but not
fussy. They were, in a word, cool. I didn't want to look like a prude.
Tonight, it would be the three of us taking on the Arena Health
Club. As they talked more about it, it began to dawn on me what
the Arena was. I recoiled a little but didn't let it show. Maybe I
would meet someone new at the Arena and start a new relationship.
Maybe there was a café where he and I would get to know each
other better before sex. I pictured alabaster white Doric columns

and plant life. An azure blue pool. Maybe this gay life wasn't so scary, so threatening, so alcohol- and drug-driven as it seemed. Maybe I could let my hair down a little. Try something new.

I talked a big game in the cab headed to the Arena. With each streetlamp that whizzed by, I heard myself make up a new story of sexual adventure. I heard myself telling them that once I showed up for a dinner party only to find all the guests naked. It was mostly men but there were some women there, I said, but I didn't care. I pretty much just fucked everybody and when I was done I smoked a joint and that made me horny again so I just dived right back on to the pile and started fucking everybody again boy that was a crazy night but that's what I'm like, you know? If I see it and it looks good to me, I'll just start fucking it. According to me, I had been involved in three-ways and orgies covered from tip to toe in genitals and there was no sexual situation that I was intimidated by.

My lips were numb with cocaine and lies.

I got carried away in the adventure of it all. I was quaking from the kind of good yayo you could only get back then. The cabdriver stared straight ahead and Tate and Jeremy barely raised an eyebrow. In truth, all night long, they only seemed to be putting up with me. I knew they didn't like me. But the more evident this became, the harder I tried. I clung to them and followed them around. I laughed too loudly at their jokes. I just hoped that my face wouldn't give away how scared I really was. And I hoped that, somehow, I could trick them into protecting me at the Arena without knowing they were doing so. I was certain that I was smarter than they were.

"You walk through the door, then you pay the man, then you get naked," Tate said as we approached the door of the club. He sounded exasperated. Somehow he knew I had never been here before. The Arena sat in the middle of a seedy neighborhood. It looked like a dilapidated old house. I walked through the door, paid the man, and then I got naked. They supplied me with a towel so small that it could only just be held around the waist with a forefinger and thumb without a fiber to spare. I could tell immediately that there would be no café. There was no spa, no Doric columns. Also, there was no workout equipment, making me question whether or not this place was really a health club. The Arena Health Club itself looked unhealthy. Ill, even. Dark and brooding with paint peeling off the walls and all manner of haunted voices coming from the dark corners inside. I stood in the entrance, taking it all in, and turned to my friends. But they were already gone. The smell of Jeremy's freshly applied Drakkar Noir hung in the air. I was naked and alone.

If you are at a gay bath house and not participating in sex, you are suspect. The man who we handed the money to and who handed us our towels barked at me to get moving. From behind, I must have looked as though I was slowly marching to the hangman's noose, the fingers of one hand straining to keep the tiny towel in place and the other straight down at my side refusing to touch anything before disappearing into the darkness. It was like walking into a funhouse. I had no idea what to expect. The noises that men make echoed all around me from unseen places. Expectations are useless when you're surrounded on all sides by human nature.

The bath house was huge. The cocaine switched up its effects on me. My heart was pounding and I was covered in a thin layer of sweat. A sweat that was making me cold.

I was surrounded by dark and seemingly endless hallways with doors on both sides. Some doors were open and some were closed. The open ones held naked men inside who wanted me to see what they were doing to each other. They looked right into my eyes as I passed, hungry for attention. A man on his knees removed another man's penis from his mouth to point and laugh at my slow and tentative tiptoe down the hallway. Open doors loud with sucking and slapping sounds. I could pick my pleasure. It was a sex museum in which I was the sole patron. At the end of the hallway was a door with celestial light emanating from it. Bright as heaven's gate. The lone man inside was on the bed, on his knees with his face turned away and shoved down in the pillow. His skin was white as the marble of a Roman statue, like the famous ones with no arms and no head. His hands were placed on each buttock pulling them apart to reveal his bloodred anus like an open wound.

I turned and ran.

I ran back down the hallway and into another where men were standing around relieved of their tiny towels, cackling with laughter as I scurried by. I ran past the salacious looks and annoyed frowns. Some grabbed for me and I jumped away, yelping like an injured sea lion. It was still early in the night and not many men had found a partner yet. When I could run no longer, I skulked through the hallways, head down, stiff upper lip, until they all eventually disappeared inside private rooms or into corners where eyes were closed and heads were thrown back in ecstasy or deeply bowed and bobbing. I walked past a large room, where seemingly dozens of men were all on one bed, all arms and legs and grunts, and I caught a brief glimpse of Tate's face in the fray under the dim blue light. His back was arched, eyes closed, head thrown back, and he was covered in hands. I expected that I would just roam the halls silently all night until my friends were done and I could go home. My safe little home. I expected that it would all be over soon.

Then I rounded a corner.

The biggest, fattest, white man that I have ever seen was standing at the end of the corridor. There was a fluorescent light flickering, shorting out just over his head. He was breathing heavily, shoulders heaving. He stepped out of the light and into shadow and took two steps toward me, his bare feet landing with two distinct thuds on the concrete floor. I could feel his eyes sizing me up for a moment. I could feel his face contort. He began to barrel toward me. Hairy, and Cro-Magnon. I stood for a moment, eyes wide and mouth agape, before I pinched up my towel tighter between my thumb and forefinger and took flight. He came after me undeterred. I ran as fast as I could run in a tiny towel. I looked over my shoulder and saw his red eyes narrowed with determination. I could hear his bare footfalls slap-thumping against the concrete and his rough panting in hot pursuit. There was no one there to help me, lost as I was inside the corridors of the Arena Health Club, a place where I had no business being to begin with. For an instant, I thought I was going to die in there. What would my mother say? How would she explain this at choir practice? I ran through the club taking dizzying turn after dizzying turn with a deranged, horny white man determined to fuck me to death right on my heels. I made a turn to the left and interrupted two men in a passionate embrace who looked up mildly annoyed and I said, breathlessly: "There—there's a man—."

They both gave me an irritated look that said, *Of course there's a man.* So I kept on running. The big white man was not giving up. He was not taking the hint, despite my full sprint in the tiny towel. I ran to the empty natatorium downstairs. The door boomed loudly as it slammed behind me. The fear of AIDS had permanently closed the pool a long time before, haunting the cavernous space with the echoes and splashing of lovers past. It was now a dry riverbed, drained of all its water and ribaldry, with all manner of detritus resting at the bottom. I hid behind a set of mini bleachers that were set up outside the pool for spectator viewing of the wet and wild fun that used to go on inside. I hid and held my breath until it burst from my chest. And I heard the telltale footfalls of a maniac thundering against the concrete. Echoing now. Just he and I. There was only one way in. There was only one way out.

His footsteps got closer until I could hear his inhalations coming raspy and heavy and I looked around frantically trying to find another escape route.

"Please," he said, in the gentlest possible way. This one word echoed, bouncing off the walls to surround me on all sides. "I saw you walking around out there. You don't look like you belong here." He waited. "Please," he said again, "I love Black men. You in here?" His voice cracked and was brittle like an old man's.

He rounded the corner where I was standing to find me hiding there. Standing right in front of me, I could see that his rough breathing was not the maniacal expulsions of a fuckdemon, but of a large man who was just having trouble moving his massive weight. He towered over me, bearded and bedraggled. He looked like every truck driver I'd ever seen at a rest stop on the turnpike. His eyes were just bloodshot, not blazing, not demonic. He seemed tired. He seemed tired of all this. He looked down at me and I started to tell him that I had no interest and that I was going to scream if he touched me. But I was not afraid anymore. Something in his sad manner let me know that he meant me no harm. What I saw in his eyes was a gasping loneliness. Pure and simple. The kind of loneliness that begs for some—any—form of humanity to reach out and touch. I saw the deep despair in the wet eyes of a big, naked trucker. He reached out to take hold of my towel and I slowly pushed his hand away and shook my head. He looked disappointed. I didn't know what to say. So, without a word, I moved past him and walked slowly through the door that I came through, leaving him and his loneliness behind.

Tate and Jeremy met me at the entrance both fully dressed and looking refreshed. I told them stories. I told them lies. I don't think they believed me. We did more cocaine. Lots more. I drank an ungodly amount and would eventually learn to live for both alcohol and cocaine and wouldn't go a day without one or the other or both. They were the two things that seemed to make me everything that I wasn't: bold and fearless. Because as far as I knew, the first rule of being a man was to have dominion over women and, since I couldn't do that, I wanted to master a different kind of manliness that was popular, accepted, and even praised as the most masculine in my tribe: that of the promiscuous drunk.

I would eventually graduate from vodka and cranberry to straight Jack Daniel's and learn to go back to the Arena all on my own. I got better at it, every time with a head full of whiskey and blow.

The Arena Health Club no longer exists. It burned to the ground under what some consider mysterious circumstances. One young man died in the fire. But I can show you exactly where it was. I can show you the exact geographical spot that sparked the end of my innocence and when the lights in my life slowly began to dim.

I would be lying if I said that I am not imagining Tuan is my son. Gazing at him, I wonder who will be the first to let him know that our beautiful dark brown complexion will make life complicated. I know it will happen soon.

When I was not much older than him — when my family had a little bit of money, when my father was working — we all once went out to eat at a breakfast place one Sunday morning. I was excited. We didn't go out to eat very often. This was a treat.

The restaurant was alive with activity. It was a small place and had a family feel. My mother had been wanting to go there for a long time. We walked in the door and a hostess greeted us with a smile and ushered us to a booth. I had never sat in a booth to eat before. I ordered pancakes and, when they came, they had a whipped cream smiley face painted on them. I decided that I would relish the moment. I cut them into little bite-sized triangles and ate them slowly, smiling the whole time.

When I looked up, there was a little girl about my age sitting directly across from me in the adjacent booth. She was the prettiest thing I had ever seen. Golden honey brown skin and freshly done braids with pink and purple beads hanging off the ends. She had big brown eyes and a button nose. But her upper lip was curled up in disgust. Her fork hovered over her plate with a bit of egg still clinging to it. She was staring directly at me.

I smiled at her and her look of disgust turned to full horror. I couldn't work out what I had done. She nudged her mother sitting next to her. At first the mother paid her no mind, but the girl nudged harder and harder and with more urgency until the mother finally leaned over.

"I can't eat no more."

"What? Your food just got here. Whatchu mean you can't eat no more?"

The girl, with her fork still midair, gestured with her head toward me.

Her mother followed the girl's gesture, locked eyes on me and seemed immediately to understand what the girl was talking about. Just to make things clearer, the girl dropped her fork on her plate and loudly whispered, "Look at that Black, ugly boy, Mama."

They knew I had heard it all. The mother shushed the girl, kept her eyes off me, covered the girl's plate with a napkin, and hailed the waitress to ask for a take-home container. This is how I learned that I was ugly. Things have changed a little. Now, I see dark-skinned men everywhere on television and in movies. But I have believed myself ugly for a long time. I don't want that for Tuan. I don't want him to have to rely on empty platitudes like "The blacker the berry, the sweeter the juice." That's what I used to say to people who said I was too black. I never really meant it, but it was the only thing I could grasp at. The only thing that made me feel any semblance of pride.

SANDALWOOD

My erection is pressing against the zip fly of my jeans. They're JNCO jeans and they're the latest thing. Everybody's wearing them, but if I'm honest, I think they look a bit silly and I feel ridiculous in them. They have wide, flared legs. You know, for dancing. They're so wide they cover your shoes and God help you if it rains. If the hems get wet, they get all soggy and heavy and, before you know it, you're drenched from the calf down. Mine are not real JNCO. I just bought a pair of big jeans at a thrift store and I wear rubber bands around my groin area to make the legs flare. No one can tell because my shirt is long enough to cover them. I don't have the money for real JNCO jeans, but when I go out on the dance floor to throw shapes, no one is the wiser. Right now though, I can tell because my erection is pressing against the denim between the two rubber bands. The cocaine I'm on is doing its work in dispatching any shame I should be feeling.

I've followed my friend, Michael, and his boyfriend, Phil, out to the parking lot of the club, where they are having sex in the back seat of a car like two teenagers. I'm watching them make out. I think that I'm a safe enough distance away, but it doesn't matter. Their eyes are closed. Their faces are obscured by each other's body parts and the windows are fogging up. It's raining, so the hems of my jeans are collecting water that is slowly creeping its way up the

pant legs while simultaneously soaking my socks. They are kissing passionately. Removing clothes slowly. They are rapt with each
other and I am trying to keep the knowledge that I am clandestinely
watching at bay. I am trying not to think of what would happen if
one of them were to suddenly look up and see me standing here.
I have a vague plan that I will just pretend that I was looking for
them to go back into the club, but I'm certain my face will give me
away. I'm careful not to catch its reflection in the car window for a
couple of different reasons: The first is that I am sure I will look exactly like the glassy-eyed degenerate I am. Second, because I don't
like to see my face.

Michael is Black too, but not Black like me. His skin is the color
of sandalwood and his eyes are light brown. He is the color of tea
with lots of cream and you can make out his features even in the
dark club and men are always asking him what he is "mixed" with. I
hear them as they rush past me in the club to whisper in his ear and
ask him "Are you Puerto Rican?" I watch as they fall all over themselves to be near him. I hang on and wait for his leftovers, desperately trying to catch their eye after he rebuffs them. They don't ask
if I am Puerto Rican. They don't have to follow me home to know
where I come from because they already know I am plain old, gar-
den-variety, regular Black.

It isn't Michael that I'm standing there for, though. I am in the
rain staring into a station wagon where my friend and his boyfriend
are doing it because I want my friend's boyfriend. Although Michael is good-looking, I have never been attracted to him. He and I
have been friends for a long time and he's like my brother. My eyes
are trained solely on Phil. Phil is everything that someone like me
dreams about. He has just grabbed the back of Michael's head to
pull his kiss in tighter and I want to step in closer and pretend that
he's holding me. Phil's last name is Italian, which means he isn't
regular white, but his skin is pale as the purest alabaster. He is sloe-
eyed with heavy lids, like a young Robert Mitchum. The corneas
are surrounded by thick, black lashes. He keeps his jet-black hair

short and his lips are always flushed pink. I covet him. I try to flirt with him when Michael isn't around. His is the face in all the magazines I take to bed with me. He is the kind of man every gay dreams about. Men like Phil grace the pages of *Blueboy, Drum, Honcho.* Physically, he is the standard. And Michael couldn't care less.

Michael and Phil aren't really "boyfriends" in the strictest sense of the word. Phil follows Michael around like a starving animal to whom Michael throws a scrap every once in a while, like tonight, for instance. Michael doesn't have any money and Phil does. He paid Michael's cover and has been buying him drinks, even though Michael isn't even twenty-one yet. Phil has never bought me a single drink, and I am twenty-five and so is he. I am far more age-appropriate. Michael's fake ID didn't pass muster with the doorman, and Phil had to pay the doorman extra to get Michael in. From the moment they passed the threshold, they started arguing. It eventually escalated until their shouting could be heard even over the thump-thumping of the bass and the siren sounds as the fight spun further and further out of control under the flashing lights.

"Why don't you . . ."

". . . just trying to have a good time!"

". . . just go home!"

". . . buying you drinks all night!"

That's all I could make out from the safe distance I'd carved out for myself at the end of the bar as the lights spun around them and Phil's expression grew more and more desperate. He was pleading with Michael to calm down, trying to get Michael to look at him, but Michael couldn't be bothered. He is petulant and childlike. Not like me. I would take every gift that Phil had to offer with gratitude. If you ask me, Michael doesn't treat Phil right. He ignores him. Avoids him. Speaks ill of him when he isn't around. Michael once told me that he didn't really *like* Phil. Said Phil was desperate, possessive, and "clingy." Said he didn't trust him. I don't see any of that when I look at Phil. It's true, I have seen him looking at Michael malevolently from time to time, but I think that must be only because he loves him so much.

The bouncer was just making his way over to break them up or throw them out when Michael threw up his hands, stormed outside in the rain, and left Phil standing there looking dejected. I wandered over to him and pretended to be a friend. I looked into his pretty white face and feigned sincerity and concern. I was delighted to be alone with him because usually he ignores me and views me only as baggage that he has to put up with in order to be around Michael. I bought us both a drink, although I had already had several and was drunk, and tried my best to make him forget about Michael. My friend.

I sat next to Phil on a barstool and faced him. I studied the lines of distress on his face and tried to think of ways that I could help smooth them out. I leaned in closer and closer and then I put my hand on his thigh.

"What are you doing?"

"Nothing, just . . ."

Phil grabbed my hand by the wrist and flung it from his thigh. He fixed me with a disgusted look. His eyebrows knitted in angry disbelief and lip curled, and he gave me an appalled once-over with his eyes. He stood up and stormed off, leaving me alone to wish that I looked like Michael with the sandalwood skin.

I crossed the dance floor, headed downstairs to the toilets, and stood outside the stall until two men came out. I went inside and opened my bag of blow and proceeded to snort as much of it with my little spoon as possible. Rapid fire. One right after the other until my head was spinning. It's the little spoon that Michael gave me for my birthday one year. Now I have an aversion to chopping up lines. It feels like a waste of time.

I sat there resenting Michael as I snorted blast after blast. I grew more and more frustrated. Embarrassed. Fists clenched. If I'm honest with myself, I would admit that I hate Michael and I don't know why. He's never been anything but a good friend to me, and I continually stab him in the back, grasping for some of what he has in Phil. But I can't help it. It's what I like. It's what everybody likes. It's what we learn to like, and I don't have any control over that. We learn that white boys are people and Asian boys are exotic and Hispanic boys are luxurious and Black boys are for sex. I have learned this the hard way each time I'm told to leave after not fulfilling a white man's fantasy. I have learned this from the white men who invite me over only when their white boyfriends are out of town. From the white men who have expected me to be more "athletic." I have learned this from every creepy-faced white man who has ever thought they were giving me a compliment by allowing the oiliest, most lascivious racism to slide from their lips.

I did almost all the coke, flung open the stall door, and headed back up to the club. I walked through the dance floor and out the front door, turned the corner, and there they both were: Michael and Phil kissing under an awning on the sidewalk with rain cascading all around them. Just like out of a movie. They've made up. They headed to the car and I waited a while before I followed them. Now here I am, soaked to the skin, watching Phil touch my best friend, wishing my best friend was me, because I am a bad person. But my dick is no longer hard because now I am thinking. I am shivering and thinking.

I am standing in the rain wondering what seized my brain early on that made me believe white men to be the only ones worthy, of being the only ones who are fully human. I am wondering who wrote this script that I, for some reason, have been so determined to play out. And now I am no longer looking at Michael and Phil. I am looking at my own reflection in the car window, dripping and shaking and desperate for white male attention as it has always been. I am watching my own face as Michael and Phil's bodies move just beyond it behind the fogged glass. I look like a crazy person. I wonder who taught me that white men were so beautiful and that I am so ugly. Who keeps teaching us that they hold more value? Is it *Blueboy*? *Honcho*? Hollywood?

Maybe it's the cold, but I am wondering what it would feel like to be as enchanted with my brownness as I am with Phil's whiteness. What if I believed brown boys to be just as worthy as white ones? I find myself wondering what it would be like never to allow another white man into my bed to steal my energy. To humiliate me. What if I stopped chasing them? Who would I be if I unlearned all the things I've learned without my permission? All the things that the darkness of my skin is supposed to mean.

I briefly consider the idea that it has never been about mere looks. People from different races look a million different ways. Maybe it has always, for all of us, been about who we consider to be more valuable as human beings. And it occurs to me for the first time that maybe I have somehow learned that Black men aren't valuable. Aren't worthy of love. Including myself.

Phil slides his hands into the waistband of Michael's JNCO jeans and starts to slide them down. Now I feel creepy. I feel every bit as pathetic as what I have been doing for the past five minutes elucidates. I feel dirty and embarrassed. I back away slowly at first and then turn and break into a run back to the entrance of the club. A combination of cold and cocaine still has me jittery, so I find a place in the corner to sit as the music continues to thump and the lights spin and the people dance. I am no longer thinking about how racist this gay life is. I am worried that Phil has told Michael what I tried to do earlier.

I will sit here for a while and hope that they come to collect me. If they do, maybe we'll stay and dance for a while. Maybe we'll have a few more drinks. They will smell of sex and dance together and smile secret and knowing smiles to one another. And I will try my best to include myself and behave as if nothing is wrong.

Tuan's father has made him sit down again and the boy seems to have noticed for the first time that there's an entire back of the bus. He is immediately fascinated by everyone behind him. He leans forward in his seat when he hears the voices of the three couples. When he catches someone's eye, he waves. They smile and wave back and he moves on to the next person. He looks deeper and deeper into the rear of the bus. He is excited to be making everyone's acquaintance.

I take in the faces of the passengers one by one, the way Tuan is doing. Some people stare blankly forward, some have their heads bowed toward their phones. I don't trust any of them. They all make me feel unsafe and nervous. It's not late enough at night yet, and there are too many people now. I have spent a lifetime looking for acceptance among these faces. I find them all disappointing. It often feels like there is no place among humanity that I can call home. I have spent a long time searching.

I used to believe, with the help of drinking and drugs, that I was a people person. Now, absent those crutches, I find people laid bare for what they really are. They are desperate for something, anything to cling to. I find that I am better off on my own, where there is no one to disappoint me but me. I want no more of the pain that people cause.

Tuan catches an old woman's eye. He waves and says "Hi!" She is having none of it. She regards the boy for a just a second before she goes back to looking out the window. I turn to look at the boy as his smile fades and his face falls into utter confusion. His disappointment breaks my heart. I turn back toward the old woman. Her morose demeanor doesn't crack, and I have to wonder if I have become more like her in this moment or more like Tuan.

LIKE THIS

Most of my nighttime encounters I will spend the rest of my life trying to forget. They all begin at bars—lonely late-night roach motels that attract desperate men who do desperate things —and end the same way: with white men rolled onto their sides as soon as the magic is over, showing me their backs, and leaving it up to me to "decide" it's time to leave, while all the excitement that existed only moments before evaporates into thin air. Then it's just a matter of getting dressed and hitting the street, invariably having forgotten a few items. A trail of my abandoned underwear, socks, cell phones, and hats litters the city of Pittsburgh, from the Mexican War Streets to the South Side Slopes. No matter where I end up, the street positions me directly under a flickering and unforgiving spotlight. It is then that I pick a direction and hope the sidewalk leads me home.

Pressley's sits on a corner in the middle of a residential neighborhood. Ugly on the outside and too small to be a bar, it is easily mistaken for just another little house in an underserved neighborhood where I was once held up at gunpoint. The place is falling apart. Dingy curtains hang in two tiny opaque windows of glass block. Brown shingles cross the façade like giant cockroaches, dividing two columns of dried blood–colored brick. In the very middle is a recessed door with a crooked sign that reads PRESSLEY 1. The door, also deep red, is shuttered by two creaky steel gates, which I swing open to gain entry. As I step up, I hear muffled talking, laughter, and music inside, but when I try the door, I find it fully locked. I tug harder. It doesn't budge. The laughter inside continues while I stand there perplexed. Then I see a doorbell glowing, moon-like, to the right of the door. It isn't possible to just walk into Pressley's. Entry must be approved. When I gently push the tiny glowing circle with my index finger, it makes no sound that I can hear, but inside falls silent.

Half a face appears on the other side of the window in the door. Its eye travels up and down my body and then up and down again before the sound of locks unbolting. The door jerks quickly open, turning loose the smell of sweet liquor and stale cigarettes. The woman inside the door is broad and imposing for her short stature. Her hair is buzzed to the scalp and her brown skin is so smooth and flawless that I want to reach out and touch it. Her breasts are mountainous, and her eyes continue to travel the length of my body suspiciously, but stop short at my eyes.

"Yeah?"

I say the first thing that comes to mind.

"I wanted to get a drink."

Her smirk is all-knowing as she takes a step back, lightly gripping my elbow with her left hand and reaching with her right to clutch the end of a black plastic paddle. Gripping it in her palm, she pushes a button on it. She goes aggressively between my legs first, rubbing it against my crotch and then all down the sides of my thighs. She tells me to raise my arms and rubs the metal detector under my armpits, then tells me to turn around and goes to work on my ass and back. She slides it against the backs of my legs and then uses her left hand to turn me around again. She looks up directly into my eyes and says without a hint of a question: "We gon' have a nice time tonight, right," then takes a long drag from her cigarette.

My words won't come out right.

"Yes. We . . . will . . . gonna."

She laughs at me with a succinct exhale that blows a burst of smoke from her nostrils and moves aside so that I can step into the dimly lit room.

"Hey," she calls after me. "You a stud or a fish?"

"I don't know what you—"

"Well, if you gotta ask, you prob'ly a fish." She laughs and shakes her head slowly as she sits back down on her stool.

I had heard that Black gay bars existed in larger cities. I had imagined them to be places where the weight of being Black and gay would be lifted. I had not found acceptance among white gay people. I had only been picked up one evening at a time to fulfill Mandingo fantasies and produce big black cock on demand. I had not found a space for myself within the Black community, either, with all of its Jesus and rules regarding male behavior. I had imagined Pressley's to be place of communion for my kind. I envisioned low lighting emanating from flickering candles atop each cocktail table and a lone bartender, handsome as the devil in a pressed white shirt, asking me what I'd like to drink and smiling broadly when I gave him my order. I looked forward to sitting at the bar, taking in the smell of incense and listening to light jazz, transfixed by every beautiful, Black male face in the crowd, in every shade of brown, all dressed to kill. They would all know one another, and their eyebrows would ask me what took me so long. As they introduced themselves one by one, I would know that never again would I have to wait in the corners of white gay bars for someone who was "into Black guys."

The interior of Pressley's punishes me for having such grand fantasies. It is nothing like I dreamed it would be: no tasteful cocktail tables scattered beneath twinkling tea lights, no décor to speak of at all. Pressley's looks like a repurposed basement, a rec room that someone's father gave up on halfway through. Directly ahead is a pool table and, behind that, the sound system. Two enormous speakers sit on either side of a cheap stereo where a man stands, occasionally changing the track on the CD. The floor is peeling linoleum. To my right, a group of people sit on an old and peeling faux-leather couch and on metal dining room chairs with ripped cushions underneath a lamp with its bulb highlighting the stained, yellow shade. It is clear that they all know one another and laugh and talk with the easy rapport of longtime friends; their eyes forbid any approach from me.

To my left is the bar: an assemblage of white plywood hammered together by someone who just wanted to establish a barrier between the patrons and the liquor. No two barstools match and a young girl with dead eyes stands behind it watching me suspiciously. I walk toward her and take a seat. I say hello and she says nothing as she slides a cocktail napkin slowly in front of me. I get the distinct feeling that she doesn't do this for anyone else. She makes me feel like an interloper. Her eyes are overly done, masked behind loads of purple shadows and tarantula lashes. Box braids sit high and mighty, cascading from the knot on top of her head. She cocks it to the side as her eyes travel down and then back up to meet mine. With every distrustful blink, she lets me know that I most certainly don't belong here. She sees right through me. Knows instinctively that I have spent a lifetime trying to prove that I am "better" than other Black people. That I'm "different." I can see in her face that she knows that I'm a perpetual user of the trick-bag of "respectability" and she is not the least bit impressed.

All I can think to do is turn it on harder. I enunciate with all the aplomb of a defense attorney.

"I'll have a Jack Daniel's neat, please." I try to sound as cheerful as possible, but her face retains the stoicism of a kabuki mask.

"We ain't got Jack Daniel's. Got Jim Beam." Her eyes travel down my fussy sport coat from the lapels to the sleeves. The crease between her eyebrows deepens.

"Oh, okay. What other brands of whiskey do you have?" I smile and look over her shoulder, but when our eyes meet, her face has relaxed into a combination of resolve and boredom. She sighs.

"Don't know. We got Jim Beam, though." The finality in her voice has decided for me.

"Ah. Well, that's fine. I'll have a Jim Beam, please. Neat. Thank you."

She strolls away wordlessly and returns to me with a red plastic cup filled to the brim with Jim Beam and ice. I don't want to make a fuss. The drink is only two dollars, so I hand her three. She looks at me, annoyed that I can't count, and hands the extra dollar back. There are a few other people at the bar; they ignore me. This is a family place and I have brought in the outside world. They turn their backs and avert their eyes. I feel every inch of my person being avoided and hear my own swallowing deep within my ears. Every movement I make is a strained effort to look more relaxed that instead makes my barstool squeak, re-announcing my unwanted presence in the room. I order watery Jim Beam after watery Jim Beam because I am afraid to leave. I don't want to walk across the room to the door, which feels farther and farther away. I stay because I know, without a doubt, that once I walk out and the door slams behind me, they will all laugh. Their laughter would confirm for me, finally, that there is no place in the world for me to go.

Only when the alcohol begins to soften the edges of the room do I notice that every couple at Pressley's is arranged butch to femme. Every male couple and every female couple who are clutched in an embrace or holding hands are mimicking the traditional roles of men and women. If two men are up against a wall, it is the bigger, broader-shouldered one who is on the outside and the small, skinny one in a tight tank top and short shorts who is backed up against it. The "masculines" are the most fascinating to me. They are the kind of men who blend during the light of day, and who would never show up at any ridiculous Pride parade that we all know is for white people and where I have wasted so much of my Black time.

You a stud or a fish? The bouncer's words come back to me as clear as rainwater. And, even more clear is the answer: I do not know.

I stand up from my stool and lean conspicuously on the bar from time to time, trying for all the world to look like a man who intentionally went out on the town alone to enjoy the music in somebody's grandmother's basement. I bob my head and sway my shoulders awkwardly to the heavy basslines that I am barely listening to, pretending to be fascinated by the few cheap paintings on the walls. I try to make conversation with the bartender, but she has made clear her disinterest in me. She refills my plastic cup frequently, but silently—only to travel to the other end of the bar and laugh uproariously with others. I'm sure I look ridiculous, anchored to a wicker stool, swaying drunkenly in a bar where an electric fence has been built up around me. The thought of leaving in defeat for real begins to take hold when I feel a presence next to me.

He just stands there with a beer in his hand, not close enough to touch, but close enough to smell. At first, he positions himself on the bar, leaning his back against it, elbows resting on either side of his torso—the way a cowhand would relax on a corral, with one leg extended. But then he turns to face me. Staring. Inches from my face without saying a word. I offer an "excuse me" and slide my barstool over a little away from him, but he follows, still staring directly into my profile. I don't need to look: I can smell the handsome on him. He smells like a new haircut from a Black barbershop. Pomade and Bay Rum aftershave and baby powder. He is breathing down my neck and, when I finally turn to look at him, I am happy that I do. He hasn't taken his eyes off me. He isn't smiling. He looks like he's mildly disgusted and genuinely curious. He is staring at my shoes.

"Florsheim," I say.

"What?" he says, finally looking up.

"Florsheim." I stick my foot out. "I got them on sale."

"Oh." He still looks mildly appalled and confused. He cups his palm over his mouth in the way someone would who is laughing at an inappropriate joke: an attempt to hide a smile that the eyes betray.

Another silence ensues. He stares at me occasionally with his lip curled and I pretend to be bopping along to the music.

"Whatchu drinkin'?" he finally asks.

"Jim Beam. I usually drink Jack Daniel's, but she said they don't have any."

"Oh."

"You like Jim Beam?"

"Never had it before."

I look up at him and feel sex wash over me. Apart from the completely confounded look on his face, he is gifted with beauty. He is deep brown and broad-featured, and his barber is a master of precision: his hair is cut close and with such symmetry that only the sharpest of blades in the stillest of hands could have done it. His eyes are deep set, which compels me to go looking for them inside his face. He looks tired.

I raise my glass to get the attention of my hateful drink-refiller and she drops an additional red cup of ghastly brown water on the bar without saying a word.

"I'm Brian."

"Jason."

He squeezes my hand too hard, crushing my knuckles. Then he takes a sip of his Jim Beam and makes a face. I laugh. He looks up immediately and I see what looks, in the dim light, to be a flash of anger.

"It's an acquired taste that I still haven't acquired," I say, jokingly, trying to show that it was all in good fun. It is only then that he smiles a little.

"I guess so," he says. "I guess it's an acquired taste."

Jason wears the male costume: dark and loose-fitting with sneakers. He takes the stool next to mine and sits down, then we both face the bar as he alternates between his beer and sips of Jim Beam. He is a man of few words. Every question I ask and every attempt to begin a conversation is met with monosyllables. I learn quickly that a "yeah," "no," or "for real?" is all I am going to get. He mostly keeps his eyes straight ahead looking at nothing in particular. When I ask him what he does for a living, he answers "this and that." I ask him the clichéd "Do you come here often?" and he answers, "Only place I go." He seems sad and deep in a way that teases my rescue and victim instincts all at once. He is complicated and maybe I am the man who can ease his spirit. But, most importantly, he is Black, so I am sure that he can ease mine. He is the embodiment of the place my two disparate identities meet. He will not debase my brown skin to a fetish.

He lets me buy him several more tumblers of whiskey before he finally looks at me directly and with heavy-lidded eyes asks, "You wanna go? I can get us a jitney and we can just go if you want." I exhale deeply and feel my penis move. I had already decided that he was beautiful, Black, and complex, and I was honored that he'd asked me. Chose me. I couldn't wait to get out of there.

"Yeah, we can go if you want."

When we get off our barstools, I realize Jason is considerably more drunk than I am. He wobbles and has trouble finding the armholes of his jacket. He takes much effort in pulling up his baggy pants around his hips only to have them fall too low again and again. His first step toward the door is an outright stumble. I grab his arm to steady him and he snatches it away. We walk slowly, with him hitching his pants up the whole time with all eyes on us. The bouncer, still sitting on her stool, looks at me. It's the only meaningful contact I've had all night. There is a combination of worry and warning hidden in the corners of her eyes, but I don't recognize it at the time. She opens the door so that he won't fall into it and says to no one in particular, "Night, gentlemen."

We stumble into the cold air and decide to go to his house in the Hill District. The jitney ride is a mausoleum of silence and I know instinctively that I shouldn't try to break it with idle chatter. The driver is listening. Jason rests his head on the rear passenger window and stares out at the city whizzing by with lights playing off his face. I know in this moment that he is closeted. I can tell by the shame that causes him to fold his arms over his stomach, hiding his hands in case one of mine errantly travels toward him. His head is resting on the window, and every breath he exhales against it is a request — a demand — to be quiet. We drive on in silence. The time is 2:15 a.m.

His home is a slum — a bedsit up four flights of stairs in a blighted section of the city. The hallway of the building is lit by ugly fluorescent lights and smells of piss and cigarettes. He opens his door and I am assaulted by the smell of mold and old fruit. Standing in the doorway, I take in the dirty carpet and industrial green painted walls and a television, replete with a Nintendo 64 game system. There is a negligible kitchen area with a mini refrigerator and no stove. Around the room's one and only window, he has strung up white Christmas lights in an effort, I suppose, to give the space a little cheer. His bed is littered with dirty clothes, and pinned on the walls of his room are photos of naked women torn from magazines. Black women in various, sexually suggestive poses: One sitting in the lotus position scooping up her left breast in her right hand to lick her nipple. One bent over in high-heeled shoes with her ass facing the camera. One just laid out bare, with her legs spread wide leaning back with her hands behind her head.

Before I can say anything, Jason grabs me and spins me around to face him. He has retrieved a beer from the mini fridge and is taking long thirsty gulps from it. Then he grabs the back of my head and begins kissing me hard with his mouth wide open so that my lips press against his teeth. It is too aggressive, too wet, too bizarre. He chews on my lips and chin in a way that speaks more of hunger than of desire. He pulls at my clothes while he maneuvers me over to the bed, thrusting with his hips the whole time. His body is desperate and flailing and, when he bites my bottom lip, the pain is so piercing that my eyes fly open and I push him off me. He looks confused. Anger and embarrassment mix on his face in equal proportion.

"It's just a little too rough," I say.

"I gotta go to the bathroom," he replies.

The toilet is communal and down the hall. I hear him slam the door and all I want to do is leave. I sit up on the bed slowly and place my head in my hands, running my fingers slowly down my face. The neighbors are having a party. Loud voices and music come through the wall as if there is no wall at all. Shame floods me as I look around the room. I stand up and look out the window down to the sidewalk at the street. I can hear it calling for me. I reach down to pull up my pants and, out of the corner of my eye, notice dozens of yellow envelopes piled up along the wall. They are from the State Correctional Institution, Mercer, Pennsylvania. All ripped open. A place filled with femmes and butches, studs and fish. When Jason returns, I will tell him all the lies the white men told me. That it is getting late. That I have to get up in the morning. That I have to let my dogs out.

He flings the door open with a bang and comes at me with all the force of a cyclone. Wet mouth and all arms. He pushes me back down on the bed, pinning my shoulders with his knees while struggling to get out of his shirt. He is telling me how much he wants me and, before I can move, he is landing tooth-kiss after tooth-kiss on my face and neck. I struggle beneath him, then press my hand against the wall and push with all my strength. This sends him toppling to the floor, where he immediately dives under the bed and resurfaces with porn magazines. When I sit up, he is at my knees, flipping through the pages like a madman, trying to show me the pictures inside and tugging at my pants.

"Look at this. Ain't this hot?" He looks up into my eyes. "Ain't this hot?"

And I can see. His beautiful eyes have gone glassy and empty as deep space. He tries to dive on me again. I push him off and begin to look for my shoes and jacket. I am buttoning up my shirt while he stares at the floor.

"Why you gotta go?" He doesn't look up to ask this question and rubs his thigh nervously with his shoulders hunched.

"I gotta be up tomorrow and—" I stand up and survey the room looking for any item that might belong to me. I step around him and begin to frantically turn over the mess of clothes, papers, and dirty dishware on his floor looking for my thrown shoe.

"Man, how can you *be* like this?" he asks. I find this question annoying and undeserving of an answer, but decide to placate him until I find what I'm looking for.

"I'm not *being* like anything. I just have to go. Where is my shoe?"

"How can you *be* like this? I don't wanna *be* like you!"

I don't hear what he is really asking, at first. But then I do. He wants to know how I can exist in the world as such an abomination. An insult to Black manhood.

"You think you can even *handle* this dick? You think you *man enough* for this dick?"

I find my shoe in his avalanche of dirty clothes and then remember my jacket. My jacket has my wallet in it. If it didn't, I would just leave it. I want to escape this place running.

"—*handle* this dick?" he says again and that's when his voice breaks. A slight crack in a dam that gives way to a flood. He cries a drunk cry that rattles his breath. The kind of cry that only bursts through when you've got nothing left to hold on to and nothing strong enough to hold it in any longer. "Why ain't you a man? Why cain't you be a man? How can you *be* like this? How can you be like this?" he asks over and over. But, now, I know that he isn't talking to me.

I kneel in a pile of dirty clothes watching a man wilt in front of my eyes. His shoulders round and his head bows. I don't remember what I say. I don't know if I say anything. I'd like to think that I say something reassuring, something kind and profound. But I don't think I say anything. *How can you be like this?* I had already asked this question of myself many years before and can't remember if I'd come up with any answers. Jason falls on his side and cries so hard that the sound catches in his throat. I sit beside him as he sings the words "faggot, faggot, faggot" to himself and, again, I know he isn't talking to me. I rub his back a little and can't tell if he even knows

I am there. When he goes quiet, I find my shoe and jacket and, as I've done so many times before, I let myself out, closing the door gingerly behind me.

On the street, cool air blasts me in the face. I look up and take in what seems like the same streetlight that follows me around the city. It mocks whores like me in the late hours. It takes pleasure in knowing that, if it has to sit outside in the dark, used and meandering, so do I. I can't take sitting at home on my own at night. Too many ghosts use silence as their time to attack. I convince myself that I am bored, when what I really want is noise to drown them out. I persuade myself that I am horny, when what I really am is lonely. So I allow the street to lead me from club to tavern to dive to bath house, chasing something that I can't quite define. But it all ends up the same disappointing way and I vow never to go out again, until the next night, when a hope-driven amnesia sets in and the street tricks me into doing it all over again. It invariably leads me somewhere, some strange man's apartment or house, and waits patiently outside for me to be spat out in short order. It would be nice, just once, to feel like I could spend the night.

The streetlamp. My spotlight of judgment. I am its star. Like always, I don't know in which direction to go, so I just choose one. I am left searching for home once again. I walk until I see people who look dangerous, hanging outside of an after-hours, and I stride past them, trying to look confident and manly in my sports jacket and dress shoes. They eye me with only curiosity. I pull my jacket around me more tightly and keep moving. The time is 3:15 a.m. and, if I am lucky, I might make it home before sunrise.

The bus has crossed the redline. This is Squirrel Hill where a lot of white people get on. I refuse to move my suitcase from the seat out of sheer principle. Squirrel Hill. The nice neighborhood. It's the first neighborhood I lived in when I moved to this city a long time ago, but I couldn't afford it and had to move out soon after. Squirrel Hill, to my knowledge, was the first time I ever laid eyes on a Jewish person or at least a person that I could identify as Jewish. The houses here are nice. The storefronts are thriving. But like every other spot in this city, bad memories are waiting for me here. They jump out of the neatly trimmed hedges, wiggling their bony fingers and shouting "Cootchie-cootchie-coo!"

Tuan has become bored and restless again. He is fidgeting and keeps trying to stand in his seat to look out the window. He begins to fuss and his father is still talking on the phone. In a move that I wasn't expecting, his father pulls an iPad out of his backpack, fiddles with it for a moment, and then hands it to Tuan. He has queued up a game. I can tell by the reflections of lights twinkling in the boy's eyes that it's a colorful game filled with distracting cartoon characters and sounds. Tuan begins to press buttons randomly and finger the screen. He can't press buttons fast enough, and the iPad is making electronic crash and bleep sounds. Each time it does, he smiles big.

But the game is more than just pretty lights. It requires skill for it to keep working and Tuan has none. The objective of the game is lost on the child. He just wants it to light up and when it stops, he hands it to his father with his bottom lip poked out. His father takes the machine from him, resets the game, and it all starts over. Tuan plays with it again, savoring the pretty lights that make his eyes dance, but his lack of strategy and skill get in the way, again leaving the game little more than a frozen brick in his hands. He can't get it going again. He hands it to his father to reset. His father resets it and hands it back. The same thing happens.

This last time, he hands it to his father who ignores him and the sobs begin to well up. He pushes it closer to his father's face and begins to cry.

"Stop cryin'."

His father snatches the game from Tuan and puts it back in the backpack and now the boy is about to lose control. His father will have none of that.

"Stop cryin' right now."

Tuan immediately chokes back a sob. He sits on it. He squeezes his eyes shut until his body complies. He swallows it. Makes it all disappear. All he wanted was the pretty lights. He didn't know that he had to prove himself for them to appear.

This will be his lot in life. They will hand him games. They will put sports equipment in his hands. They will force him to perform and perform well. This will be expected. They will hand him bats and balls and introduce him to hoops and bases and helmets. Tuan doesn't have long before he is expected to transform into what they think his body is fit to do.

Many years from now, men that Tuan doesn't even know will approach him on this very bus and try to strike up conversations about sports.

"How about them Steelers?"

My father was a man like that. It was out of genuine concern that he handed me a baseball glove and insisted on playing catch with me. He pulled me outside to stand with him in the autumn air where we faced one another like gunslingers in a fast draw. He looked at me with question marks playing up a crease between his coal-black eyebrows on his coal-black face, wondering how I could possibly be something that he'd had any part in creating. He stood with confident feet planted firmly on the ground, whereas I took a more relaxed approach; hip thrust out to one side with the giant glove on my right hand. I held it up to my face like a fla-menco-dancing lady holds her fan.

This moment was, to my memory, the first time I had donned such a glove. A dead thing on my hand. But I liked the smell of it very much.

Summer was taking its last breaths and the sky was the color of erased pencil on white paper. I was delighted because the air was cool enough for me to wear that darling faux leather jacket that I loved, topped off with a smart, powder blue knit cap. I wasn't paying attention to my father's words as he spoke to me. He was speaking in that foreign tongue he only used with my brother that, at eight years old, I had already learned to tune out.

Other sports yielded similar outcomes. I was intrigued by all the wrong parts of it. Basketballs, for example, are resilient things. I've always been fascinated by how something so innocuous-looking could take such constant punishment. Footballs introduced me to one of my favorite new words as a child: oblong. My father kept handing me these balls, hoping to conjure a miracle. But they were just air pushing back against a leathery prison. Air doing its best impression of a Black boy in America.

I was doing my best impression too, playing catch with my father. I remember thinking that he was doing ballet at first. His hands rose slowly up to a praying position under his chin and he leaned unnaturally backward with one foot remaining stubbornly planted on the ground. The other foot coiled and curved up, gracefully bent at the knee, rising higher and higher until it seemed like he would topple over backwards. He was so graceful, my mouth hung open.

His hands separated. The right hand extended all the way behind his head and his whole body commenced to lurch forward. The leg that was bent at the knee made an audible thud against the wet grass in front of him as it hit the ground, and the rear leg extended behind him. My father's normally stocky, grimy, and clunky frame was lithe as liquid and refined as teatime. I was so transfixed by his beauty that I was caught wholly unaware when the angry ball collided with a crack against the bridge of my nose. It was the kind of pain, dull at first, that grows more intense with time. It didn't immediately dawn on me to cry, but after a few seconds, the tears came in torrents accompanied by bouts of shrieking. It didn't hurt yet, but I cried anyway. I cried and cried the tears born of wondering why he would ever do such a thing to me.

I wonder what ball Tuan's father will put in his hands.

WE STRIKE STRAIGHT

THE KEY

He leans down close at The Holiday, one of my go-to bars, and whispers in my ear, "Do you play basketball?" The softness of his voice tickles my earlobe. I look up at him from my barstool.

After he asks, he leans back and folds his arms as if he already knows the answer. He bites his bottom lip and lets his eyes run the whole length of my body until they meet mine.

"You must play basketball."

I can see that he's already picturing it in his mind's eye. He is already picturing me on the court in matching shorts and jersey, posed with the ball in a jump shot. He is tall and I detect a foreign accent, but cannot determine where it's from. He has seen American basketball, he says. I am afraid that he will start to talk about it using specifics to which I cannot respond, but he only seems to know players' names. They are names that I have heard before and so just knowing who they are seems to be enough for now. His eyes are pale blue and set behind blond lashes and fixed on me as if I am everything he has ever been looking for. He is a graduate student come to America to teach math at the university and his accent is dripping with sophistication. He is the kind of man who doesn't belong in a seedy place like The Holiday. I have only seen his likes in movies. He hails the bartender and turns to me.

"What would you like to drink?"

"Jack Daniel's. Neat."

When my drink arrives, he leans on the bar next to me by the light of the jukebox. He is now talking about specific basketball teams and I cannot fake any knowledge of this, so I put my hand on his leg to distract him. His prosthetic is a surprise to me. He shifts it away stiffly and searches my eyes for signs of flight. I show none. He is easily the most handsome man to ever take an interest in me. He helps himself to the barstool next to me and continues to speak of basketball. I lean in and let his accent wash over me amid the din of a filthy bar and feign enthusiasm, knowing full well that I have no earthly idea what he's talking about.

"How often do you play?"

I deepen my voice to its most masculine timbre and bless him with the only basketball lingo that I know. I lower my head and lift my eyes to meet his before I smirk. "Oh, I've been at the top of the key more times than I can count."

He is already fascinated and leans in closer.

They called that space on the gym floor where I nervously stood with the ball "the key." I had also heard it called "the paint" and "the lane." The key is where boys stood on either side of me at the basketball hoop like two firing squads when it came time for me to try to shoot the ball. They didn't even show me the courtesy of a blindfold. Even if one of them had walked up behind me and covered my eyes with a pitch-black handkerchief, tying it tight in a knot behind my head, it couldn't make my performance inside the key any more appalling. The basket may as well have been a dozen miles away and a hundred feet high. The ball, that cornerless and slippery bane, would never drop inside of it when launched from my hands. I threw like a bitch, they told me. I threw like a blindfolded bitch. I didn't quite know where to place my feet or my hands. I tried to watch the other boys when they did it with seemingly no effort. I tried to mimic them. Even when they missed the basket, it still looked elegant and they would all, in unison, sing "Awwww!" in a "better-luck-next-time" chorus that solidified their friendships and underscored my ostracism. They trash-talked each other in a competition that seemed to reward those who could be the funniest through cruelty. They did not "Awww!" when I missed the basket. They just laughed. Bent over at the waist and holding their bellies. Heads thrown back pointing fingers at my failure. They laughed until they cried, some of them. Couldn't catch their breath. They had a name for this torture. They called it "free throws." But they weren't free at all. I paid dearly for mine.

At the top of the key, I tried to hoist the basketball just over my shoulder and bend my wrist back like they did but I couldn't have looked on the outside the way that I looked in my head—as the laughter from the edges of the key would begin to percolate. I tried to bend my knees in the way that I saw the other Black boys do: ever so slightly. They giggled. I tried to bounce up and down on the balls of my feet a couple of times the way that they did. They snickered. The coach would cover his mouth and let his head drop to his chest and, upon seeing that, all pretense and holding the laughter in would cease. I would bounce the ball once on the gymnasium floor and then pretend to be measuring up my shot. I wasn't. I was panicking and steeling myself inside for the onslaught. I was killing time until the inevitable launch where the ball would go flying just about anywhere that wasn't remotely near the basket. It would take off like a hawk whose hood had just been lifted into the great beyond and parts unknown. It would either barely make it to the basket or go past it. The sound of my ball hitting the backboard was an unrealized fantasy. It never went in. Not even once. And then, because the other boys were so busy laughing, it was my job to go and chase the ball down. As I did, I could hear the gym teacher ordering them to stop laughing through stifled laughter of his own.

I dreamed of the day when free throws and hoops and backboards would no longer be a part of my reality. There is no place more like hell in the world for an uncoordinated and unathletic Black boy to be than under the gaze of other Black boys inside the lane, the paint, the godforsaken key.

His name is Bertrand. He pronounces it in a way that I cannot mimic. We sit at the dark bar together over a twinkling candle like lovers, leaned over it with torsos twisted so that we can stare deeply into each other's eyes. In his, I see cool pools of infinite blue and, in mine, he sees basketballs. He reaches under the bar to hold my hand and stroke my fingers with his thumb to test them for length as he smiles at me. He keeps his blond hair cut short and his face is a perfect, smooth oval.

I ask him where he's from and he sighs heavily with boredom, leaving me to wonder how and by whom he's been asked this question before. He recites the answer to the question while rolling his eyes.

"I have lived in England, France, Germany, and Switzerland," he says. "I don't want to talk about that," he says. "Americans, they always exoticize me and ask silly questions."

I feel dumb for asking such a pedestrian question and decide to keep it to myself that I've never been any farther than Detroit. But he is not interested in that anyway. He is preoccupied with taking in my body.

"How long have you played basketball?"

I tell him that I have played since I was a kid, which is or isn't a lie depending upon how you look at it.

The eagerness in his eyes tells me that I should backtrack. Softpedal it. So I look off into the distance and adopt a philosophical and serious tone. I fix my eyes on the EXIT sign over the bar door and allow it to help me to craft a lie—a lie born of the knowledge that I have acquired over the years: that these white gay men love their Black men to be the kinds of Black men they see on television, in their sports, in rap videos. Manly and unflappable. They like big Black bucks, hardened by racism with graceful bodies chiseled by sports. I will lie because I don't want to lose him. Because I want to show him that I am worthy. I think back to gym class and try to channel what the boys who played basketball well must have felt. I conjure up every memory of every basketball player I ever glimpsed over my brother's shoulder as he watched them being interviewed on his television sports shows. The lie I tell is ridiculously dramatic.

"When I play ball, I just feel free, you know? I feel like I can forget my problems and just focus on playing the game. I can just let go of all my stress."

He leans in close enough so that I believe I can feel the heat from his body. His head hovers out of focus in my peripheral vision but I can *feel* him listening. He releases my fingers under the bar and rests his warm hand on my thigh.

"I get caught up in the action of it," I continue. "All I can think about is getting the ball to the hoop. It just becomes, like . . . *necessary* for some reason, you know? I really can't explain it and if you don't play the game it's hard to understand, you know? I just feel, like, *electric* when I play ball. There's nothing else like it. I just love being caught up in the action of it all."

I did not soft-pedal it. He falls silent for several moments while the music and chatter of the bar drones on around us. I have laid it on too thick. I shouldn't have said that "electric" nonsense. I am certain that, if I turn my head, there will be a look of incredulousness on his face, one eyebrow raised with a smirk. So I don't look over. He begins to move his hand up and down my thigh slowly and he is still taking in the side of my face. The EXIT sign is looking more and more inviting.

"Would you like to go somewhere else?" he asks me.

I turn to him and his face betrays the fact that he has just fallen in love. His expression has gone serious and concerned. A deep crease between his eyebrows.

"I know," he says, "that you have pressure in America. With ze racism."

I agree to go somewhere else and we both know where that somewhere else is going to be. As we head toward the door, he tells me that he knows all about American racism and that it disgusts him. Europe is far more advanced. He is happy that I have basketball to relieve my tension from the ignorant white Americans. As he opens the door of the bar, I think back to the last time I actually held a basketball. I remember how I hated it when we would play shirts and skins. I remember the techniques I employed to get myself through it.

The trick was to lag behind the group. The boys chased the ball around like a pack of dogs, all huddling together, and their every movement was dependent upon its travels. They held their hands in the air to block other players from seeing the ball's movements. They shuffled and shifted their bodies quickly, making the gymnasium floor squeak beneath their footfalls. And always shouting.

"I'm open!"

"Over here!"

They followed it intently with their eyes as they wiped the sweat with their T-shirts and only glanced at one another to assess whether they were threat or ally. He who had the ball was the focus of all the attention, and so I just decided that I would never have the ball. I stayed far enough away from the pack to ensure that it would never come to me, not even accidentally. So I lagged behind the group. When they ran to one end of the court, I would follow them slowly at a jog that was basically a walk. I did not "hustle" for the ball. No one wanted me to and that suited me just fine. I only wanted the hour of Phys Ed to pass as quickly as possible, but it never did.

The only thing I learned in Phys Ed was that my body would never do the things that it was supposed to do. My body was the worst bully that I'd ever had. It swished. My hips and wrists were too loose. My hands found their way to my face far too frequently, wrists glued together under the chin with fingers fanned out across the cheeks. My shoulders were never more than an inch from my earlobes, tense like they wanted to force the body to be as small as possible. I flounced and lumbered effeminately. Any attempts to appear more skilled were met with uproarious laughter. I tried to make my body be forceful and tried to get it to compete. But it disobeyed. It was a marionette with tangled and impossibly knotted strings. So me and my body followed behind the boys, close enough so that it might look to a passerby that I was part of the game, but far enough away to ensure that the ball would never come to me. I straggled for the duration of the games, steeling myself for the very worst part of the class, the moment when my body would betray me the most. And when the gym teacher blew his whistle to signal that class was over, I knew that the worst was yet to come.

Bertrand takes off his leg when we get back to his apartment. It is jarring at first. He sits it in the corner and it watches us like a sentinel as we make ourselves comfortable on his mattress on the floor. I try not to look at the place where it is amputated. Mid-thigh. We begin to kiss in a less frantic way than I am used to in these situations. We peel our shirts off slowly and with purpose before we both lie back on the mattress. He uses his hands too roughly against my skin, pressing against the flesh with seemingly all of his strength. He speaks in a foreign language that, to me, makes the entire encounter seem less like we're lying on a floor mattress in a messy apartment. I do not know what he is saying, but it makes me feel romantic. I stand to remove my pants and he is looking up at me smiling.

They started to make us take showers after gym after puberty raided our bodies and we all began to stink. I never worked up a sweat and didn't see why I should be made to shower. I pleaded this case, which fell upon the gym teacher's deaf ears. Everyone had to shower. The English teacher who had us after gym class had made it clear that she couldn't take the stench anymore.

So we were made to get naked in front of each other and given no instructions as to how to maintain our dignity. I lagged behind and took extended drinks from the water fountain. I opened the door of the locker room to a blast of steam and a chorus of hoots and hollers. The boys took to communal nudity like ducks to water. They reveled in it. Jumped around making their penises bounce. They did horseplay as if they had been naked in front of each other for their entire lives, like they had never worn clothes before. I sat down and slowly removed my shoes. There wasn't a lot of time for me to get wet enough to pass the test. Mr. Seifert would be in at any minute to check. I rolled my socks down and removed them painstakingly, as if they were fused to the soles of my feet. I forbade myself to look up. I kept my head aimed toward the cement floor and breathed in the smell that so offended that English teacher, but made me feel dizzy. Repugnant and inviting to me at the same time. I tried to hold my breath, which resulted only in my having to inhale a potent blast of it eventually. The smell was wet earth, sour but with a perfume underneath that I could not identify but that captivated all my senses. I would sit there and smell it all day long if I could, and I inhaled it with my head swimming and undressing as slowly as I could because the body I was using was betraying me even as I sat there. I could feel it wanting to make public what I had worked so hard to keep in private. I was terrified to look up. Their faces would know what I was thinking. But I didn't know what I was thinking. I couldn't trust my hands for fear that they would do something without my consent, like they did almost every night. Quiet so my brother couldn't hear. My body felt recalcitrant and evil. So I made my way through the steam and stared down at their bare feet, all with toenails in need of clipping. Boys were disgusting. I turned the water on as hot as I could make it. I took the towel with me to cover my midsection. My mother would ask me later why the towels she sent me to school with came back so wet. Most of the other boys would leave as soon as I entered. I stood under the water for as long as I could and tried to scald the thoughts away. It never worked. But I stood there trying desperately to wash away thoughts of sex.

My hand only grazes the place where Bertrand's leg has been taken. I want to look down and take it in. I want to see it, but it would be rude to look. Instead, I look down and take in the whole scene. One leg where it should be and, beside it, an absence. He tells me how firmly I am built. How manly and strong. "I would love to see you play basketball," he mumbles through lips entangled with mine. "I would love to see you on the court. You are probably amazing." His breath comes faster as he talks about it. His eyes are closed and his head thrown back against the pillow. "I would love to see you play," he says again. I am swept up in his pale beauty, coasting on a wave of lust that makes it easy to lie. I plant kisses down his neck and on his torso as I assure him. "You will," I say panting. "You will."

The white boys generally ignored me at school. Once it was determined that I was in no way able to increase their cool factor, they left me alone. They ignored me like they ignored the Black girls. They had no use for either of us. It was the white girls who got all of the attention. The pretty ones. I caught myself on occasion wishing that I were one of them. I wanted long, flowing hair and alabaster skin. I wanted to be loved the way that they were loved by everyone, especially the Black boys, who couldn't seem to keep away even though the unspoken rules about that sort of thing were clearly established.

But the Black boys hated me. They seemed to think that I was somehow tied to them. Representative. They despised the way that I made them look. They wanted everyone within earshot to know that I was not one of them. I was a birth defect. Their cruelty outshined that of even the white kids at my school. They were compelled to distance themselves from me at all times. They wanted everyone to know that.

"He a faggot."

Glenn Banks was turned around backwards in his seat on the bus. I looked up to see him smiling malevolently and pointing the entire bus's attention toward me with his accusatory finger. His hair hung loose and greasy in its Jheri Curl.

"He a faggot, y'all. Y'all should see him in gym. Don't nobody even wanna shower cuz he be in there."

A couple of girls snickered. And Glenn took this opportunity to press further. "He run like a bitch. Even Mr. Seifert be laughin'."

At this, there was more snickering. Anger welled up in me but was quickly mixed with shame. Every muscle tightened against what was sure to come next. My face went numb and all I could hear was the whoosh of the blood inside my head against the laughter that was now rising.

"Hey, Brian. You a faggot? Is you?"

He asked like he really expected me to answer. "Is you a fag?"

I looked up again hoping to give him an angry look that would deter him, but whatever I managed to produce on my face didn't derail him in the slightest. He asked again, looking directly unto my eyes. Challenging me.

"You a faggot, nigga?"

I scanned the bus. Some kids stared down at their laps with embarrassment for me. More were looking right at me with their mouths agape waiting for me to answer the question. Or fight. I did neither. Near Glenn sat my brother, whose eyes were cast down. He didn't dare look up. Glenn was his friend. They played basketball together. For a moment, I believed that he would spring into action and we would both take on Glenn together and that would be that. After we beat him, I would never have to face this kind of humiliation again. But he just sat there, overcome with the mortification of even knowing me. Glenn continued until he got bored. When we got to our house, the bus stopped and let me and my brother out on our doorstep. He turned his head towards me and glared with a boiling hatred, his fists balled up at his sides. He flung open the house door and stormed inside, leaving me there to watch the bus roll on. A sob caught in my throat and I swallowed it. He hated me. Black boys hated me. All of them. From my father to my brother to Glenn Banks. They were all a source of pain and, much like my Judas of a body, the basketball, and the key, I wished I could be free of their demands.

Bertrand has asked me to meet him for a date in Squirrel Hill. The good neighborhood. We have been seeing each other on and off for about a month. He is terribly busy, and I try not to bother him, but when he calls, I am elated. He wants me to meet him at the cor-

ner of Murray Avenue and Hobart Street. I wear one of my masculine outfits. A tight-fitting T-shirt and baggy jeans that all but cover
my newly purchased adidas tennis shoes. I know that he likes this.
I look the part. My body is muscular like an athlete's. As I'm scan-
ning the street, guessing which restaurant we might be going to, I
see him come around the corner looking radiant. The sun, which is
setting behind him, has been playing with his hair, making it paler
in some places, darker in others. He has tanned since the last time I
saw him, and my mind is already racing with thoughts of later when
we are alone. His prosthetic leg gives him a peculiar gait, but I can
detect a bounce in his step. He is wearing a large backpack. As he
gets closer, I can see that he's smiling at me with all his teeth — a
smile so singularly focused that it makes his blue eyes squint. No
one has ever been this happy to see me. He gives me a full kiss on
the lips, which I don't mind him doing in Squirrel Hill. He grabs me
by the shoulders.

"We are going to play basketball."

"Excuse me?"

"We are going to play basketball. There is a basketball place here."

I look around and see no "basketball place" and then look back at
him smiling, sure that he is joking.

"I don't know of any . . ."

"It's just up here on Hobart Street."

He is exhilarated and already walking in that direction. I follow
him, still uncertain of what's happening. He is talking at a rapid
pace and walking quickly with his slight limp. He's waited so long.
I lag behind as he chatters about seeing my moves. Just ahead, I
can now see what he is referring to. The picture comes into full
focus. We are approaching a playground — the kind of playground
they have in rich neighborhoods with colorful swing sets, sliding
boards, and seesaws all placed carefully atop soft sand. It's the kind
of place with kelly green tennis courts marked off with stark white
lines with stark white people running back and forth. It's the kind of
playground with pristine and smooth basketball courts, unmarred

by cracked pavement. He stands at the entrance and smiles back at me.

"You know zis place?"

"Yeah. I've been here a bunch."

I am still lying. I have been lying for a month. I have been putting him off for weeks. It never actually crossed my mind that this could actually happen. It was all just talk. I told him that I was sort of a star on my high school basketball team. I fed him my brother's life with all the awards and accolades that he received. I told him of an injury that I'd never sustained. I filled his head with stories of how I was "too competitive." I look around the courts and see that there is a group of boys already engaged in a game. Anxiety is creeping its way up my back and my ears are starting to ring.

"I don't wanna cut in on their game," I explain. "It looks like it's already in full gear."

"Zis is no problem," Bertrand says. He reaches inside his backpack and pulls out what looks to be a brand-new basketball and holds it aloft. Its burnt color and black ribs temporarily blot out the sun. He tosses it to me with his chest and I catch it holding it away from my body like a baby that's soiled itself. He starts over toward a park bench and it is then that I realize that Bertrand doesn't want to play basketball with me. He wants me to play basketball *for* him. I take a deep breath and try to think of a way out of this. I shout at his back about my injury and he tells me to just "take it slow." He just wants to see my moves.

He sits himself down on a bench so that he can watch my Black athleticism. My Black athleticism will turn him on. I bounced the ball once hoping that it would cooperate. It returned to my hands dutifully and promised to behave itself. I thought for a moment that maybe I could pull this off. Maybe, after all these years, my Black basketball gene would show its obstinate face just in time to save me from looking a fool. I bounced the ball again. Again it returned. I turned to the hoop and all hope drains from my body. I tried to toss it.

It is as if the basketball wakes up and realizes that it is caught in the hands of the exact wrong person. It pitches in my grip. Falls backward when it's meant to go forward. I try. Oh lord, how I try to make that thing behave. The ball, desperate to get away from my incompetence, rises up against me with a petulant hatred. It bounces between my legs, causing me to look backward after it and go chasing it down the court. Once caught, I accidentally kick it, hunched over in a ridiculous display of ineptitude. I kick it, chase it down again, and attempt to hold it aloft in my best "I meant to do that" pose. I launch it toward the basket in a foppish toss and it bounces away and I chase it again. It jumps from my hands again and bounces toward Bertrand, who is looking more and more distressed with each fumble. The ball has it out for me, wants no part of me, and twice strikes me in the nose. I cannot dribble the ball without looking at it. I don't dribble it, so much as I slap it to the ground over and over again. I cannot walk and slap at it at the same time. It escapes. It entangles itself between my feet. If the ball had a finger to point, it would have directed it right at me doubled over laughing. The ball calls me "faggot" again and again until Bertrand has had enough and with a disgusted look on his face yells . . .

"Stop! Just . . . *stop!*"

I pick the ball up and place it under my arm at my hip. Even after this disastrous performance, I am still trying to play the athlete. I hand him the ball. He is annoyed and doesn't look me in the face. He returns the ball to his backpack and looks over my shoulder at the other boys who are playing basketball. He has asked me to stop for my own good, before they could see me. He slides the straps of the backpack over his shoulders and begins to walk away. I follow him dutifully. We go to dinner at a Korean place. I try to make conversation. His responses come infrequently and with monosyllabic clarity. He is behaving as best he can for a man who is obliged to feed a con man. When the check arrives, he pays it, then we get up and stand at the door of the restaurant together. I can already see his mind working. He does not wish to go with me anywhere else.

I have torn down the walls of every fantasy he constructed. I am a liar. He is struggling for an out, avoiding my eyes and looking out at the street. I won't beg him. I've been here before. So I do what I do best. I lie.

"I have plans to meet some people for drinks at Pegasus tonight if you want to come."

"No," he says. "I don't want to go there."

I didn't think he would. There is no kiss this time. No hug. He lays a hand on my shoulder, says good night, and disappears out the door. I already know not to call him anymore. There is a bar on the other side of the restaurant. My body walks toward it. It's the only thing it ever does on its own that makes me feel any better.

After my brother and I got off the school bus, he lets the screen door slam behind him. I stood on the stoop of our house with Glenn Banks's words echoing through my brain.

"You a faggot, nigga?"

I sat down on the step and asked myself the same question. I had to tell myself the truth. I knew that I could never be what they all needed me to be. I wondered why God had done this to me. A worm has found its way from the soil up on the concrete step to wiggle beside me. I open my palm and flatten it with my bare hand, relishing its death and feeling its guts explode. I turn my palm up and look at the mess, the tiny life I was able to destroy.

"You a faggot, nigga?"

Yes.

The couples at the back of the bus are moving now toward the front. They stop in front of Tuan and his father to say their goodbyes. The men once again grapple with their firm and robust handshakes and the women all focus their attention on Tuan. He takes the opportunity to charm them again. They laugh and bask in the joy of his cuteness.

"Byyyyyee Tuaaaaaaaaan!"

They all make their way to the front door as the bus nears their stop. The feeling of jealousy rises up in me again. The woman in the jean shorts has her hair cornrowed sideways. She is popping gum like firecrackers inside her mouth. She reminds me of my old friend from the mini-mart Denise. Same hairstyle, same full figure, same gum popping, same lyrical laugh. When Denise thought something was funny, the music in her laugh would comfort me in the late hours when we worked together. She wouldn't let up until she left you in a pool of giggles too. And she was beautiful. Dark brown skin like the woman standing before me now and a smile that could drive away dark clouds. I wonder whatever happened to her. I left her standing outside that mini-mart in the wee hours of Akron, waving at me, and I never once thought about thanking her for saving me that night I was undone by my roommates. Denise saved my life without even knowing it, as Black women often do. She saved it without me even asking.

The woman in front of me on the bus who reminds me of Denise looks back and catches me staring. She makes a sour face. I look like I am checking her out. Even if I was, I am far too old for her but I try to smile anyway. She rolls her eyes. I suppose that's fair. I'm happy that she's found love.

For Black women, love is often hard to find and I think about the many ways in which my father and other Black men try, instead of loving them, to bring them to heel.

I have laid my problems at the feet of too many Black women. I have asked them to do too much of my emotional heavy lifting. Looked to them for counsel, to support me, to fix me, to change me, to help me feel better, to save me from myself like it's their responsibility. And to shield me from the truth.

The bus stops and lets the lovers off in Oakland, an area of the city where I kind of fell in love once. The woman with the sideways cornrows takes her boyfriend's hand and she and her crew all strut off down the sidewalk. She doesn't look back.

GAME THEORY

Ainchou even gonna take those off?"

I can tell from my position that she has asked this question to the ceiling. She sounds exasperated. I don't know what she's referring to. I am as naked as I can be and so is she, what with me having removed her panties with my teeth like she asked. She is on her back with me on top, my head hidden between her inner thighs. We couldn't be more naked.

I look up between her legs and can't see a thing from behind the foggy force fields that are my spectacles. She is now looking down at me through the valley of her thighs and waves by wiggling her fingers, suggesting that I've forgotten that she's even up there. Her brows are knitted. Her exasperation is quickly turning to concern. "You okay down there?"

Without removing my hands from her buttocks, I push my face into the bed and shake my head rapidly in a "no" motion that's only meant to clean my glasses on the sheets. She takes this the wrong way.

She sits up quickly and snatches my glasses off my face.

"Boy, gimme those." She pauses for a long while and then sighs. "Yeah, it's not working for me either."

We are both twenty years old. She is my girlfriend.

I met her at a college in Akron. I ran away from that place. But she stayed on. She is gorgeous and smart and her skin is softer than anything I've ever touched. When I met her, she was the roommate of a friend of mine and I knew that I just had to have her. For what, I'm not sure. But she ticks all the boxes: Her skin is as dark as mine. She speaks proper English. She is feminine and small. I'm lying, but maybe I don't know that I'm lying.

She and I have been kissing all day. Kissing is easy. Her lips are inviting and plush. We kissed on the campus of the college in Oakland in front of a large phallic building called the Cathedral of Learning. We made out in full view of everyone and I was wrapped in a warm and relaxing normalness that I have never felt before. Black man. Black woman. In perfect harmony.

I held her hand as we walked down the street and I basked in all the tacit looks of approval that we received from the people walking toward us. I squeezed her hand tighter. Maybe a little too tightly. She wrested it from my grip, smiled and said "easy." Perhaps she mistook my grip for love, but it may be that I was clinging to something else entirely.

We strolled the sidewalk in a Jewish neighborhood under one umbrella, like out of a movie, and an old man with a deeply Yiddish accent stopped to tell us that we are a "*Such* a good lookink couple!"

We are.

I kissed her in front of him to seal the deal. He smiled his approval of our young Black love. Everything is just as it should be. I want to do this all day. I want to be her protector. The father of her children. My voice is deeper when she is on my arm. My shoulders less rounded. I feel like I could fight.

"Vhat a good lookink couple!" the man yells at our backs as we walk away waving our goodbyes.

But we can't walk around all day. She is only visiting for the weekend and we will need "time alone together." We have never had any "time alone together." Most of our relationship has been over the telephone. I have suggested everything in the city to do to stall for time. She has eaten and walked and sightseen her fill and now she is ready to see where I live. She has a look in her eye that I have been dreading. A look that signals a reckoning.

The sky opens up with more rain on our way back to my apartment. We run, dodging raindrops under that single umbrella, but inevitably get soaked to the skin. There are thunderclaps that start out far away and get closer and closer as we run. There are lightning flashes that seem to land mere feet from us. Everyone on the street is running for their lives. I am running faster than she is and she has to stop me. She has to pull me back.

"Come back! I got the umbrella!"

We are laughing and splashing in puddles until we get to my front door where the gutters on either side of us are pouring like waterfalls as we blow out plumes of steam from our mouths, panting and gasping. I put the key in the door and hear the loud "click" sound that it makes, signaling our salvation.

It is dry and quiet inside but we can still hear the muffled rain outside. It's a little chilly inside my shabby apartment but she wastes no time removing her wet clothes. She takes off her shoes.

"This is a nice place." She looks around, not really meaning that.

She makes her way to the bedroom confidently, as if she's always known where it was. She is pulling at her blouse.

I enter the bedroom behind her a few minutes later.

Her blouse is stuck on her head because she hasn't undone the buttons. She has trapped herself, arms over head as if in a straitjacket. I attempt to help her escape.

"Wait . . . move your . . ."

"Hold on . . ."

"Hold still . . . you're making it worse."

When she is free, she looks into my eyes and we kiss. She is wearing a white bra, which glows in the burgeoning moonlight against her pretty brown skin. She drops her pants and steps out of them and toward me in one motion. We kiss and I wrap my arms around her. I am fascinated by her breasts against my chest. I am fascinated by how soft she is all over. I am fascinated by how small she is. But all I am is fascinated.

We fall into bed, kissing, and I begin to remove my clothes because I guess that's what you do and I am waiting for something to happen. I'm waiting for Sex to take over. And I feel nothing apart from the action of removing my clothes and now my skin is clammy. She feels nice and warm next to me and I wonder if this is all there is to it. But I keep kissing her, hoping that something will kick in, and she is writhing a little with her head thrown back and pushing the top of my head down further and further until I arrive where she wants me, and I look at the space between her legs where I am once again . . .

Fascinated.

I am fascinated by nothing but the spectacle of absence between her legs. The sheer "not there" of it all. She is hot between her thighs and smells like the earth and I know what I'm supposed to do now. So I dive in. I slam my face in like I'm bobbing for apples and she taps me on the top of the head.

"Gentle . . . gentle . . ."

So I pull back a little and I look at it and I stick my tongue out a little but this isn't enough.

"More . . . more . . ."

So, I try to find a middle ground but her gyrations are becoming slower and slower and I can't tell if this means I'm doing it right or not. I place my hand beneath her buttocks so that she knows I mean business, but I'm not getting much of a response. So I pull back and I look at it. I look it square in the face and decide that I will conquer it. I kiss it. Then I pull back and look again. I kiss it again and pull back. She has stopped moving altogether. I keep going but I can feel her enthusiasm dying.

"You okay down there?"

I look up and she is a blur behind my smeared glasses.

She tells me to "Come up here." I do. I lay beside her on the bed and she looks down at my dick and just knows that it has been checked out the entire time. I ask her.

"You want me to try again?"

"No. Every time I look down you lookin' at my pussy like it's made outta math."

She turns over on her side away from me and I play the outside spoon.

I hope down to my bones that she doesn't think it's her that's the problem. It's me. I'm the problem. I am a liar.

We lay in silence for a while until I break it.

"You warm enough?"

"Yeah."

"You want some more blankets?"

"Yeah."

I cover both of us in blankets in my one last attempt to be her protector, the father of her children. Normal. I ask her "What do you want to do tomorrow?"

She snuggles her butt up closer to me and sighs before she answers. "I don't know. What do you wanna do?" I know that there will be no more hand holding. No more kissing. No more putting on a show. I search my depths for an answer that isn't a lie.

I don't know what I want to do tomorrow. I honestly and truly have no idea.

Tuan's father's phone rings again. I immediately know who it is. But this time, the tone has shifted. Tuan's father answers and is speaking in gentle tones. He leans back in his seat and takes up the posture of a man who is trying to work out a problem the best way that he can. He crosses one arm over his chest and holds his shoulder. I can tell that this conversation will be the making up after the fight. He is silent more than he talks now. He agrees more than he disagrees. He is making an effort to understand her, to listen to her.

I wonder if my father ever really listened to my mother. I wonder if they ever actually had a conversation about anything other than money. I never once saw him take anything she said seriously. Anything she said was relegated in his mind to the ramblings of a woman. Anything she liked was foolishness. Her anger was dismissed as hysterics. Whatever she did had to be completely focused on shoring up his confidence and alleviating his insecurities. There is nothing sadder than an insecure man foisting his insecurities off on everyone else because he is unable to process them, to be an adult about them, and ultimately to deal with them. I know because I have been that man myself too many times.

I don't think my father ever listened to my mother or trusted her. He was far too concerned with the role he thought he was supposed to play. In the end, his need to be a "man" cut him off from everything worthwhile in life. I wonder if my mother might have been able to love him if he had let that go. But in the end, he only disappointed her. I could see this clearly even when I was a boy. I saw Black women all around me who were disappointed by their men, who felt dominated by them yet unprotected at the same time. So, I promised myself at a young age that I would never be a disappointment to my mother.

Tuan now sits, bored and disconsolate. But like any child, his recovery skills are remarkable. He moves on to the next thing with gusto, this time babbling what sounds like a tune. It's random. It has no discernible melody. But it's a song. He's babbling "Bah, bah bah" as his father is still talking on the phone. I want him to sing louder. He does.

"BAH BAH BAH!"

Tuan has now begun to dance. Lifting his arms up and down with each "BAH" and slapping his knees. He jumps a little in his seat and the "baaaahhs" become more elongated. More melodic. And louder. He wants to be seen and heard and now, finally, his father takes notice. He bends over to whisper loudly in the boy's ear: "Be. Quiet."

Tuan only needs to hear this once. His song evaporates into thin air. He inhales deeply, puffs out his chest, and releases it as a sigh. His joy has been tied off. Sutured right at the start.

A HOUSE IS NOT A HOME

I got to stay up late on February 20, 1982. I was twelve years old and it wasn't really so much that I *got* to stay up late. It was more that I just got swept up in all the excitement and nobody really noticed whether I had gone to bed or not. That night, my mother was in a state that I had never seen her in before. She was positively incandescent. Her persistent state of exhaustion and rather gray demeanor were replaced by an aura of pure orange and yellow and she was jumping about, all smiles and high kicks.

By 10:00 p.m., the whole house was alive with women and girls from all around the neighborhood wearing pajamas and fluffy slippers, their hair held high in curlers and wrapped in gossamer floral scarves. They had all been summoned by my mother. Some brought liquor, some brought snacks, and they were all in a fever of anticipation. Through it all, my father sat grumbling on the couch, arms folded and mumbling something about the silliness of women. But he couldn't complain too loudly. He could make no claim that he had to be up early in the morning for work. Back when he was in control of the house, an impromptu party like this would never have sprung up in the middle of the night. But those days were long gone, and he had no choice but to mumble sexist insolence just loud enough so that the assembled women could hear him talking, but not make out the words. They didn't care anyway. My father had disappeared for all of them long ago.

I didn't know what all the fuss was about either. I only cared that I wasn't being told to go to bed and stood in the midst of all the frenetic feminine energy in our home. The women gossiped and cackled at one another's jokes as they ran back and forth to the fridge to refill their white wines. They talked about "He" and "Him" in the same way they would be talking about Jesus the next morning. And "He" was going to be on TV tonight and they waited with bated breath for 11:30 to strike. Our Magnavox was ready.

Of the members of my family, my mother was the one who had the absolute least use for the television and dismissed most of what went on behind its thick pane of glass as "foolishness." She had no interest in what we watched, never monitored it, and walked by the set like it was an intruder in our home. It ruined her décor with its ugly boxiness and she walked around it as if it were a blood stain at a murder scene. The only time I ever saw her turn it on was if she was home in the late morning so that she and Mrs. Scott next door could talk on the phone while they watched *The Young and the Restless* together as they both cleaned, gossiped, and drank coffee. But, after the show was over, my mother used her knee to push the protruding "off" knob and went about her day. She was of the strong opinion that there were far too many white people on television. White families, white private investigators, white people in space. And, if you should ever happen to glance at one of our people, he was a troubled kid in need of help from white people: a jive-talking idiot of a bug-eyed stereotype of one kind or another. She was convinced that any Black person debased enough to appear on television was an embarrassment to the race.

But as the women gathered in our house this night, she cast furtive glances at the television, checking it to make sure it was still working. Excited. They made popcorn and laid out on the living room floor, or they sat close on the couch, waiting for the start of the show. I couldn't begin to imagine why this show captured the attention of my mother: *Saturday Night Live.*

My mother was a good, Christian woman. She typically had the same views of modern music that she had of television: all foolishness. I had tried on several occasions to try to get her to listen to Kool & the Gang and Duran Duran but she dismissed it all as "noise." Her heart was at the church and from there is where all her music came. But when she heard Luther Vandross, something in her spirit changed. His tenor transported her to a place of romance and fornication. His ballads seduced her into closing her eyes and raising her right hand in a praise move that I had only seen her execute at First Baptist Church. His more upbeat numbers made her dance, which she had never done before in my presence. He made her dance behind the vacuum as she was pushing it, and seeing that for the first time made me remember that, at some point, my mother was a girl.

I knew every page in our family photo album by heart. Inside were old photos of my mother when she was young, photos of a completely different woman. One in particular always held my attention: a faded photo of my mother and aunt in their early teens posing in a comically sexy way for the camera. Each with one hip thrust out and making smoochy faces, hamming it up. Both their heads are thrown back with hand on hips. They were beautiful. Now my mother never smiled. Just a few years after the picture was taken, my father and my older brother, her first child, would wipe that smile right off her face and begin her long ordeal of Black men demanding, needing, and taking from her, killing all her girlish dreams. But when she listened to Luther Vandross while vacuuming, I could see that young girl clearly as she raked over the same spot in the carpet repeatedly and spun herself round and round to "Never Too Much." With the opening strains of the guitar, she was transported from all her drudgery to a place of romantic, suave, and devoted Black men; a place where a million days in their arms was never too much. His voice provided temporary relief from her reality of Black men who were tired, angry, and distant. Men like her father. Men like my father.

I didn't know their story when I was a child. I just knew that they were nothing like the parents who lived inside our television. They never kissed, barely touched, and went whole days and weeks without speaking to each other. For years, it had all the appearances of an agreed-upon partnership based on his "good job," and once that was gone, all the pleasantries went with it. If there ever was a spark between them, I never once saw it. Luther Vandross's voice was the husband my mother should have had. Everything she'd ever wanted in a man was tied up in his vocal cords. He sang, "A thousand kisses from you is never too much." He allowed her to dream and let the thoughts of a real man, one who's tender and strong, wash her clean away from this man living in her house who railed against her job and complained that she was working so much even though he brought nothing to the table.

My parents had argued about money earlier in the evening, and after it was over and he stormed out, my mother began to angrily and absentmindedly rifle through the TV Guide magazine. She immediately jumped from her chair and went to hollering. "Oh Lawd! Luther Vandross! Luther Vandross gon' be on TV tonight!" She snatched up the phone. She had only ever heard his voice and seen his photograph on his album cover. I had studied the photo extensively. In it, he is tugging playfully at the flaps of his leather jacket to show his stark white dress shirt and black tie. He is handsome. Looking up at the camera, smiling, eyebrows raised enough to wrinkle his forehead and a boyish smirk tickling the corners of his mouth. A tuft of fur at the tip of his chin served to shape his face. I stared at his photo for long stretches of time and smiled back at him and it made me feel dirty and wrong afterwards. I didn't know why. I just knew that there was something about the man that I liked, accompanied by a nagging and almost imperceptible knowledge that I shouldn't.

"That voice!" my mother screamed into the phone. "I wanna see the *man* that voice come out of!" And she invited every neighborhood woman to our house to watch the show that night.

When the show finally started, with its wailing saxophone and cheering crowd, a hush fell over the living room. The man on the TV announced that Luther Vandross would be the musical guest and the women all raised their glasses in an uproarious cheer.

As my mother sat on the couch with her friends waiting for the show to begin, my father sat in a chair nearby, his face contorted with the kind of animosity that can only come from a man emasculated. She glanced at him and dismissed it, ignoring him like she had the commercial break.

Saturday Night Live began with a series of comedy sketches that my mother and assembled company didn't find remotely funny. They talked through them until the white actor who was hosting the show appeared in the lower left corner of the screen alone in front of the studio audience. Just over his shoulder was the musical guest's silhouette, the band moving just enough so that you could see the occasional flash of light off an instrument, and the outlines of three backup singers who wore pink pantsuits with fringe.

The women in my house clutched pillows to their chests, waiting for The Man Himself to step out into the light. There was a tape in the VCR already whirring. My mother was rapt. I was sitting just at her knee looking up, and she was holding a potato chip midair as if she'd forgotten how potato chips work. Her eyes were wide with anticipation, calf muscles stiff and ropy, knees together, sitting straight up on the couch. The women in the room were forgetting their husbands, their husbands with their lost steel mill jobs, hunched shoulders, beer bottles, and confusion about who they were now that they could no longer provide. These women, who all had to join the workforce in the place of Black husbands who'd been told they could never be anything other than hard laborers in a town which now had no labor. These men, who no longer held the deed to their own once-boisterous laughter and sat around in the streets like dried bush bean husks and complained, got angry because they didn't know what else to do. My father stared over at my mother from his armchair and mumbled something about women being "ridiculous." But he watched her with the look of a grieving creature; one who had lost any claim to calling himself a man.

The host announced, "Ladies and gentlemen, Luther Vandross!"

The lights came up on the *Saturday Night Live* stage. Our living room had never held such anticipation. Each neighbor lady's mouth was slightly agape. And when the music started up, I immediately recognized the first strains of my mother's favorite tune, "Never Too Much." I had watched her dance to it so many times with the vacuum, even when the floor didn't need to be cleaned. She began to tap her foot when she recognized the song too. And then, as the camera fell on the man who had embodied all their Black-woman dreams, utter confusion, outright disappointment, and naked disgust began to slowly creep through my living room.

The man with the golden voice was pudgy, his face rounded and double-chinned. He stood there as a testament to what lies photography can tell us. He wore a black jogging suit—far from the tuxedo covering a mass of muscles that the women in my living room were expecting. He was not handsome. He was zaftig and dumpy. The floodgates of ridicule flew wide open.

"He fat!" My cousin broke the ice.

"He don't look like nothin'!" There was laughter all around except for my mother. She still sat straight up, the potato chip still frozen in the air, halfway to her mouth. I was the only person in the room who wasn't looking at the television. I looked directly at her.

It wasn't shock. Every woman in the room was doing shock. My mother's face turned from what was a half second of hopeful expectation to confusion. Then her dropped chin slowly closed and the corners of her mouth softened until the lips pursed. But her eyes told most of the story. As her body deflated, she blinked slowly as if an old and familiar friend was walking toward her from the distance and was just coming into view, a friend that she didn't want to see.

For a second, she cupped her forehead in her hand, a move as if she should have known better. She was snapped back into the room by the gales of mocking laughter. Luther Vandross had begun to dance.

"Look how he dance!" a neighbor laughed, pointing to the TV with one hand and covering her laughing mouth with the other. Luther Vandross swayed his hips in a decidedly unmasculine fashion. His shoulders followed suit and his head had a tendency to bob to the rhythm in a way that was off-putting. His face was womanly and pinched. But it was his hands that most destroyed any modicum of manliness. They were far too limp and animated. He smiled like a beauty pageant contestant. He was the opposite of James Brown, who tore up the stage with testosterone. The more animated Luther became, the more emotion he transferred to his song, the worse it got. The room rose up against him. He was ugly and effeminate. The women were no longer paying any attention to him and opted instead to make fun of him to one another. My mother joined in, but the smile that had been playing with her mouth for the last few hours went into retreat, and her face took on its usual look of a freshly cleared dance floor. I could tell instantly that she wanted everyone to go home. Yet another Black man had dashed her hopes. She felt tricked one too many times, was unforgiving about it, and let the words fly.

"He look like a sissy."

And there it was.

That word I knew so very well. It was hurled at me at least once a day, seven days a week. At school, at church, on baseball diamonds where I didn't belong. I sat between my mother and Luther Vandross, knowing now that she hated me. Or would soon. Because deep inside, I knew why I stared at his picture. I knew why I never danced with my mother behind the vacuum. Somehow, I knew that I danced like this faggot on television and I knew even before I saw him that she wouldn't like it. And when I saw him dancing in those few seconds, I thought that, if my mother liked him, that she would like me.

The party broke up, with women grabbing wraps and bottles and mumbling about having to get up early in the morning. My father looked at them, pointing to the television and slapping his knee. He called Luther Vandross a "gal boy" and soaked up every drop of my mother's disappointment. This Rubenesque, mincing man on television had not only broken up her party, but made my father feel somehow manly again. The beauty and strength in Luther's tenor had all been a lie and he could tell that, just beneath her joking, my mother felt like a fool.

I thought that, maybe if my mother and I were left alone to watch Luther Vandross, she could see the beauty in him; find something she liked. Find something about *me* and my girly ways that she liked. But she was done, already showing the last guest out with a "See you tomorrow, girl."

The television was still on, but she had lost all interest. She and my father performed their nightly death march to their bedroom and, without turning around, she told me not to stay up all night before disappearing behind the bedroom door. "We got church in the morning," she said.

Alone in the dark, I sat as close to the television as I could. I wanted to see him again. I needed to know why they all hated him so much.

He look like a faggot.

I knew what that word meant too. A boy who likes boys. It was the word that hounded me every day at school. And now I knew that my mother hated them. It confirmed what I had been slowly realizing: that I needed to hide myself. I was twelve.

The host appeared again.

"Ladies and gentlemen, Luther Vandross."

I moved closer to the television to further examine what not to be. The stage, this time, was virtually empty except for Luther in a spotlight. He sang the ballad "A House Is Not a Home" and the music washed over me so sweetly that I placed my hand on the screen. I moved closer still, until I could see the speckled rainbow pixels that made up his face. He kept contorting his mouth into different shapes to make the right sound come out. Teeth against tongue, lips against teeth. I knew that, no matter how sweetly he sang, that he would never be a man and most definitely not a Black one. He was another disappointment to Black women everywhere. A dashed hope. And I knew that, someday, I would be too. I would devastate my mother just as he had, but in a whole new way. The portly man singing so beautifully to me, live from five hundred miles away, had something in common with me. I pushed the thought away and buried it deep. I was too afraid in that moment to say even to myself that I knew what it was.

Tuan's mother says something over the phone that makes his father laugh openly.

Tuan's father gets the boy's attention and hands him the phone. "You wanna speak to ya mama?" Tuan smiles and grabs for the phone, but his father won't let him hold it. He puts the phone gently to the boy's ear as his mother begins to coo into it. I can't hear her, but I can sense what she's saying.

"Hi, Tuan! How's Mommy's boy? Mommy loves you!"

The boy is now smiling and saying the word "Mommy" over and over again into the phone with such glee that my heart can't take it.

I catch myself smiling and staring at the little boy now talking to his mother on the phone and I am cheering him on. "Talk to your mother," I whisper to myself out loud like a crazy person. You will never know your own origin story as well as your mother does. She knows you better than you do. Talk to her. Because I found out so much when I finally stopped judging her long enough to let her speak.

LET THE CHURCH SAY "AMEN"

My husband don't like me coming to church. He pretty well hate everybody in here. He can't watch me while I'm here. He don't like it when I talk to other people or have any kinda life outside the house, and that's partly why I come. To get away. Talk to some people. Get a break from his fussin' and complainin' all the time. I swear if that man wasn't fussin' about something, he wouldn't have nothin' else to do. I sit here in this pew and enjoy the sunlight as it comes streaming through the windows and the paper fans get to fanning and I can feel the Spirit. Maybe the Spirit is freedom.

When I'm at home, I don't feel at *home*. I joined every organization here at this church. The adult choir, the usher board, the Ladies Guild. Just so I don't have to be in the house with him. I used to make all my kids come to church every Sunday too. I made sure they was in Sunday school and in the junior choir because I want them to grow up right. Because I know what sin is and I know how it can ruin a life. So I fought them into jackets and ties and buttons and bows and made sure they come here to get the Word. The two oldest ones done got too old for me to fight them into the church anymore. They put up such a fuss that I just eventually stopped tryin'. I got three kids: a boy, fourteen; a girl, twelve; and another boy, eight.

I like to hear my youngest boy Brian sing in the choir here. He sittin' up there now. He the only one I can still make come to church, but I don't really have to make him. He come all on his own because he like to be with me. That boy can sing. He put his heart and soul into it. His eyes squinched shut and belting out a heavenly vibrato. The song they give him to solo is "Soon and Very Soon" and he sing it so good. When the piano player start the intro, I can just about see the electricity run through his body when he take the microphone. He look just like his Daddy. I hope he don't turn out to be a liar like his Daddy. But men lie. That's what they do.

But, I ain't so innocent myself. I did what I did, like you do when you young, so ain't no use in me complainin'. Sometimes the life you had laid out for yourself ain't the life that was intended for you to have. They say everything happen for a reason and my story ain't no more special than the next woman's is. We have to navigate through men in order to have any kinda life and sometimes you do that successful and sometimes you don't. Sometimes you find yourself in strange waters dashed up on the rocks, and then you just have to make do. Every woman I know done had to navigate since the time we was little girls and Black girls get set out on the most dangerous waters.

I came up north on a train to Ohio when I was eleven years old, straight from the Georgia woods. It was like a whole new world up here. Daddy had sent for us, although I really couldn't tell you why. Maybe somebody told him it was the right thing to do. He had left me, Ma, and my sisters down South a long time before, and I couldn't tell you why he sent for us to come up here if you pointed a gun to my head. Once we got here, him and Ma stayed together for about a week and then we barely saw him after that. I don't know what that man was doing with his time. He never gave us no money. When he was around, all him and Ma did was fight, and when I say "fight," I mean just that. If you hit Ma, you better had expected to get hit back the same or worse. She wasn't the one to just stand there and let herself be hit by no man, and maybe that's why he tried to run her down with the car that one time. Maybe he figured if *he* couldn't hit her, then the car was the next best option.

After he tried to run her down, she got up off the ground and he went for her and she went for him and they whupped each other's behinds. Busted lips and broken teeth. They fought like they wanted to tear each other into pieces. She took every blow he dished out and gave back just as good until her strength ran out. But that's just the way it was back then. There wasn't nobody for her to call for help, really. You either fought back or got beat, maybe even killed.

The bottom line is that they just didn't like each other at all and I had to wonder how they ever got together in the first place. I guess he figured since he didn't like her, that he didn't have to provide for the children he helped her make. Gettin' a nickel out of him was next to impossible. I don't know what would drive a man to not take care of his kids. Even though they was technically married, he didn't even live with us. And that left it up to Ma to bring money into the house. She started doing washing and cleaning for white people in Newton Falls. She started selling homemade dinners out the house. She even got a license to do it. What she didn't have a license for is that likka she sold and she went to jail a couple times behind that. Drunk people was in and out the house all day and night. It was like a, whatchamacallit, a speakeasy. Ma drank too. She was dead drunk every day and I guess that just come from the stress of it all.

You just can't rely on men and Ma didn't. She did what she had to do and even though she wasn't no model of the Christian woman, she always made us kids go to church. She didn't know exactly *why*, mind you. She just knew that good girls went to church and, even if she didn't go herself, she made us go. So that we could grow up right. Maybe she thought it was too late for her, but not for us. But I won't hear nobody say nothin' bad about my mother. She was a good mother. I think she was just sad and the drink was the only thing that took that sad away.

I didn't wanna be sad like that.

Right after I got outta high school, I took off for the big city. Dayton, Ohio. I have to laugh at it now because we really did see Dayton as the big city back then. A cousin told us that there was good jobs there, and me and my friends Ida and Gracie took off to be single girls in the city. It was all so glamorous. We all got jobs at Rike's Department Store. I was the umbrella girl. I sold umbrellas and stood there in my pressed dress not makin' no money unless it was rainin' outside. I have to laugh about it now, the way we was playing at grown-up. Me and Ida and Gracie found a rooming house to stay in that was owned by Hasty Chatham, a round, light-skinned woman who musta been half white. She had real good hair. Just because she was light-skinned don't mean she was mean, neither. But she wanted her money on time. It was the first time I ever had my own room in my life. And we went to work and we met boys and we had us a good ol' time. Single girls in the city. But a city boy know how to spot a rube in a minute. A city boy know when that slick talk will work. And it sho 'nuff worked on me. I was only nineteen years old.

The reverend is talking about the wages of sin right now and I know about that all too well. Maybe the wages ain't exactly death like dying. The wages of sin can be a spiritual death, a prison, a life derailed and unrealized. I know about the wages of sin, pastor. Preach on.

I didn't know what I was doing back then. I was just a girl, but I thought I was a woman. I hadn't even had that many boyfriends. I dated a local boy for a time before me and Ida and Gracie decided to leave town. That's all I knew. Local, country boys with muddy boots who all worked at the mill if they worked at all. That's why I was so outdone when William Davis from Dayton, Ohio, started payin' attention to me. He was a big ol' tall, lanky man. Just arms and legs everywhere. He was handsome. He had a beautiful smile and he had his own business. A dry cleaners. I hadn't ever met a Black man who had his own real business. Not selling barbecue out of a split barrel. Not selling white lightning out of the back seat of a old truck. He wined and dined me in ways that turned my silly head. I put him off for as long as I could before he sweet-talked me into doing what we wasn't 'sposed to be doing. His words was so slippery, but they seemed so real at the time. But I didn't know nothin'. I didn't know that men will say just about anything that come to they head when all they want is to please themselves. And it's like the reverend say right now. The wages of sin is death and when I found out I was pregnant, I sho 'nuff thought my life was over.

Three of us girls went to the big city and two of us came back pregnant. When I told William Davis, all he did was offer me some money for an abortion. I didn't believe in that. I still don't. After I told him no, he couldn't get ridda me fast enough. I didn't tell Ma for weeks. I was tied in knots, but I just kept going to Rike's to sell umbrellas every day like everything was normal, and then one day she called me.

"Come on home."

That's all she said. Somebody had told her or maybe nobody told her. I still don't know how she knew. Sometimes I think it was just a mother's intuition. But no sooner did she say it than the tears fell and I was packing a bag back to the same little town I had been so thrilled to leave behind. And when I got back, Daddy wouldn't speak to me. Not so much as a word. He totally shut me out. I didn't think about the irony of it at the time, with him having left us down south for Ma to raise and his eternal stinginess and how he wasn't ever around. It just hurt. But now I think he sure had some nerve not to speak to me. There were different rules back then and a judgment over a woman for her sin was more severe than a man's. Men expected to sin. Then they take they sin out on women. So Ma and Aunt Mary Emma went to work to make sure I was taken care of. To make sure that the eyes of the community didn't fall on me with judgment and scorn. They went to work to correct my mistakes. They wanted me to marry Junior.

"He would make you a *good* husband!"

That's what they kept saying. I had never given Junior so much as a second thought. He was just another country boy to me. I had seen him at a few parties and he was a good dancer and that was it. But he had a good job working at the mill. That's what they kept telling me. He wudn much to look at. Short. Squat. Bug-eyed. Dark-skinned too. Black as midnight. Not that I got any problem with that. I'm pretty dark too. But he was real dark. Midnight Black. He wudn much to talk to neither. Didn't have a thing to say to hold my interest. He didn't ever think about things the way I did. I thought he was boring and ugly. I was vain.

But Ma said he had a good job and I can understand what with all she went through why she thought that was the most important thing. And after all is said and done, you gotta pay for what you did in the end. Everybody do. It don't matter how young or pretty or smart you think you are. You gotta pay for the dirt that you do, either here on earth or in the hereafter. But I didn't like him. Not one bit. Thought he was "beneath me." I gotta laugh about it now because ain't no way I shudda been judgin' nobody from my position in my condition. But Lord knows I had no feelin' at all for that man in any part of me. But I let them talk me into it. Ma and Aunt Mary Emma said that it was the best thing for me to do, so I married him.

We got married in the backyard of Ma's house in the summertime. The whole neighborhood came, and if you look at those pictures from the weddin', you can see that ain't one person smilin'. Least of all me. Everybody look like they just been to a funeral. I look like I'm hypnotized. Just in a daze in every photo. I knew in my bones that marryin' that man was the wrong thing to do, but sometimes the wrong thing is the only thing. I wanted to run, but I couldn't. So I decided to try to make a life with this man I didn't love, didn't hardly even like.

After the weddin', Daddy came around and decided to speak to me again. He even gave us a little house to live in because he knew we was gonna need it. What they call a "shotgun" house, and he doted on my first little boy when he came. Bought him things and even gave me a quarter or two every now and then. I just spent my days with the baby and don't ever let anybody tell you that that's just joy all the time. I lost what little sense of myself I even had. Junior worked nights at the mill and slept and ate and I watched the baby and that's just the life we had. Just a year before, I had been in the big city living the high life, and now here I was with a husband I barely knew and a baby who barely knew me. It can make a girl feel alone.

But Ma visited. She doted on the boy too and made life in that house almost bearable. She taught me everything she knew. Told me never to wake up the baby for any reason because that's when he was "growing." Showed me how to hang curtains in that ugly house. But then she would leave and it would just be me and the baby. Then Junior would come home. And things were expected. Cookin' and cleanin', I could do. But him lingering in the bedroom doorway with that look on his face was just something I didn't wanna face.

I didn't want him to touch me. But that's part of what a girl in my position had to do. I didn't like his hands on me. It didn't feel good. He was rough and clumsy at the same time.

There's just some things you don't talk about. You just don't. I think maybe he knew, he had to know that I didn't wanna be there. He had to feel my distance. He musta known that I dreamed about escape. And that's when that man started lying for real.

It's time for a selection from the choir, but it's not my boy singing yet. His voice is high like a girl's still because he so young. When he sing, it make the whole church say "Amen." It makes me proud.

When I think about how my children got here, I can only say that sometimes blessings come in the form of heartache at first. I can't say that this is how I envisioned my life would go. I had plans that were sprouts that never had a chance to grow.

There ain't no sense in goin' on about it now. But Junior lied so much that I couldn't begin to separate the lies from the truths. He kept me confused on purpose. He lied about things that didn't even need to be lied about sometimes. He lied about things that was important too. He connived.

"I can't have no kids."

That's what he told me after my oldest was born and I believed him. I just flat out believed he was telling me the truth because why would somebody lie about that? He didn't give me no doctor's note or nothin', I just believed him and I tried my best to keep him happy. He was good to the baby and he had a good job. But the wages of sin had killed me inside, and I didn't have no emotion for him. So he told me that he couldn't have kids and then when I got sick, I thought I was dyin'. I couldn't figure out what was wrong for the longest time, until I went to the doctor. What shocked me more than the pregnancy was this man's ability to lie. To look you right in the face and tell a bold and ugly lie. Right then and there, it was clear to me that I had no idea who I was sharing a house with. Right then and there, I knew that I was right in the middle of the biggest mistake of my life.

He went crazy when I tried to confront him about it. I had never seen nobody act like that before. Screaming and spitting and carryin' on. He told me that he *never* said that he couldn't have kids when I knew that that's *exactly* what he told me. He tried to make out like *I* was the one who was lying. He said I was crazy, but I knew that I knew what I knew. But I just gave up and accepted what was to come. A new baby from a man who was a stranger to me. And a conniving stranger at that. We never talked. There were no romantic moments. No laughter between us. We never shared anything about ourselves. It was all just such an *arrangement* and I was the unhappiest I had ever been in all my born days. And another baby was on the way.

The very first job I ever had was as a maid at that motel out on Route 5 when I was a teenager. Cleanin' up after white folks ain't no kinda way to feel good about yourself. Plus they just talk to you any old way they want to. I was sixteen years old and Ma had to sign for me to be able to work, which she was more than happy to do. She cleaned up after white folks, and so would I and that's the way that went. But just between you and me, I dreamed about bein' a nurse. Mind you, I didn't know nothin' about bein' no nurse. I liked the uniform all white and clean and professional. I even thought about bein' a teacher for a while, but all the teachers I ever saw was white. Besides, I didn't feel like I was intelligent enough to teach nobody. Little did I know at the time that you had to be plenty intelligent to be a nurse. I just couldn't see past the uniform. Every once in a great while, I would see a Black nurse and my mouth would drop open. I didn't know colored women could be nurses. That's what they called us back then. *Colored.* It even say "colored" on my birth certificate. That word always struck me strange like we was supposed to be white, but somebody took a big crayon and colored us in, bein' real careful to stay inside the lines. Like somebody took something perfectly white like a nurse's uniform and sullied it with all different shades of brown and black. I never liked for nobody to call me colored. But I wanted to be a nurse, and I dreamed about it while I was in that hotel cleaning nasty white people sheets and picking they wet hairs out the drain. But some dreams you just keep silent. We didn't have aspirations like Black folks do now, becoming doctors and lawyers and whatnot. But I still sometimes wanna wear that uniform. The nurses' guild here at the church get to wear the white uniform and I'm thinkin' about joinin'. All you gotta do is learn CPR in case somebody fall out into the aisle with the Holy Spirit or faint dead away at a funeral and might need resuscitatin'. Maybe I'll do that. I always wanted to be a nurse. But by the time the second baby was born, all I could do was be a housewife. Sometimes, I think Junior planned it that way.

I just busied myself with wifely duties while I carried around two babies that I was tricked into. I made friends with the next-door neighbor lady. We canned vegetables together and gossiped and watched our stories on TV. I devoted myself to cleaning house, the cookin', the shoppin'. Things that I thought a wife should do.

But me and him never talked about nothin'. We just played our roles and no love passed between us. Not then. Not now. Some of the things he do might look on the outside like love. But it ain't love. It's somethin' else entirely.

So I was standin' in the checkout line at the Miracle Mart one day like you do. I got my cart fulla groceries and the babies. Normally I don't pay no attention to all that stuff they got waitin' for you to buy at the last minute at the checkout. They try to trick you with the "impulse buy." I learned that early on. But I was standin' there so long that a book caught my eye. It was wunna those "self-help" type books like bored white women buy. I couldn't tell you what the name of that book was today if you put a gun to my head. But all over the cover, it had words about "realizing your full potential" and "gaining control of your life." It was one of those type books. Somethin' about that book intrigued me and before I knew it, I had thrown it in the cart and bought it. I guess maybe somethin' in me thought I needed it. But I took it home and started to read it and it had some decent stuff to say. I read it for a few nights and just left it on the nightstand by the bed like you do.

Next night, I go to reach for my book and it ain't there. I know I left it there but it ain't nowhere to be seen. I tore the house up lookin' for my book and couldn't find it nowhere. Anyway, I guess I forgot about it until a few days later when I went to take the garbage out. Somethin' caught my eye at the very bottom of all the eggshells and coffee grounds and whatnot. There it was. My book. My heart like to sunk to my stomach. Ripped to shreds. Pages tore out and crumbled up. It wouldn't surprise me nah bit if you told me he had ripped it up with his teeth. Tore it apart like he hated it. Like he was tryna kill somethin' dead. I stood there and stared at it for a while with my mouth hangin' open in shock until I just closed the lid. There wasn't no point in askin' him why he did that. We never talked about it. I just let it die. I let all of it die and just made a mental note about who I was married to. I fought back the tears. He had gave me another reason to look at him different. Another reason to be afraid.

My second baby was a girl. Cutest thing you ever did see. He was happy with a girl. His first born. He liked havin' a girl. He fell in love with her and played with her and praised her every move. Seem to me that men only happy with the female sex when we just girls. They want us to stay girls because they don't like grown women. They don't like us at all.

I love to hear my Brian sing. But you won't catch me fawning all over my children. White folks got plenty time to tell they children how wonderful and special they is, but that's not how I was raised. A Black child need to learn discipline in this world because if they don't learn it, they end up dashed up on the rocks. In jail or dead or worse. Ma and Daddy showed us they loved us by takin' care of us. Makin' sure we went to church and stayed outta trouble. I ain't never heard "I love you" not one time from my mother and father and that's just how it was. You take care of 'em and you make sure they do right is all. Junior was raised the same. His Daddy was the meanest man I ever did meet. He beat his kids. I whup my kids when they misbehave but he *beat* his. Knocked 'em clean across the room bloody. You don't get coddled in a Black family.

The third baby was just a case of me doing what wives have to do, I guess. We didn't use no contraception. Lord knows I hated havin' that man on me. But it was just somethin' I had to endure. But when this child here came, I swore I wudn havin' no more babies. I asked Junior if I could get on the pill and he said no. A wife had to have her husband sign back then, but I didn't tell him that. I had to trick him. I told him some ole story about havin' to sign somethin' or other and he can't hardly read anyway and then I went and got myself on the pill and then I had what they call a tubal ligation. I didn't even ask him if I could. I ain't havin no more babies for this man and that operation the only reason I'm not sittin' here with seven or eight babies right now. I didn't wanna get no deeper in the prison than I am now. He only give me so much money. He only allow me so far from the house. The only time I see people is when I'm in this church. And when I started to lose people, it all got so much worse.

Ma died in a nursing home and she was only forty-six years old. Scleroderma. I still don't know what that is to this day. I have never looked it up. But if you asked me, I'd tell you she drank herself to death. Daddy died a few years later of a brain hemorrhage at his own birthday party. After you lose yo ma and daddy, you feel like you just alone in the world. I had my sisters, but they had their own lives. One moved away and the other was busy being even younger than I was, single and free. After Ma and Daddy died, the walls just closed in and the loneliness took over.

Every night, Junior would go off to work and be gone till the mornin'. After I put the kids to bed, there was nothing left to do. I don't know why I started letting an old boyfriend from high school call me on the phone. We would stay up and chat and he just helped to keep the loneliness at bay.

We would talk until the wee hours about nothing or everything, and I won't lie and say that I didn't flirt. I talked to that man in my marital home on my marital phone that Junior paid for and that was wrong of me to do. I won't lie and say that we didn't start havin' an affair. I just wanted to feel young and free again. And I was lonely.

Late one night, I was on the phone with him just talkin' about nothing when I heard a noise and it just about stopped my heart. I jumped up from the couch and went creeping towards the front door where the noise had come from and right there lurkin' in the doorframe was Junior. All silhouette against the nighttime. He just stood there for a second and I stood there with the phone in my hand and my mouth hangin' open. My first thought wasn't about the phone. It wasn't about anything except for wonderin' why he was there. What was he doing home when he was supposed to be at work and I just stood there lookin' at this ghost in the doorframe until he spoke.

"I caught you."

Them words rolled out of his mouth all calm and cold and mean.

"I caught you."

I have never seen a man move so fast. He lunged at me with the full force of his body and I dropped the phone to the floor and screamed. I screamed for somebody to help me. I didn't have no time to run. He grabbed at my arm and held it in the vice of his hand and he dragged me. He just kept shoutin', "I caught you," over and over again and shakin' me up. I screamed because I hadn't ever seen that man act the way he was actin' in that moment. I screamed and I heard my kids start to wake up, and I tried to tell him I was sorry. I tried to tell him that I needed to go see about the kids, but he wasn't hearing a scream or a word or any of my pleadin'. He dragged me kicking and screaming out the front door.

He forced me out the front door and dragged me into the car. I told him that I didn't wanna go nowhere. But I figure that he had already planned that he didn't want nobody to see or hear what he was about to do to me. I told him I didn't wanna go but he dragged me into that car and drove away and all the way in the car I told him over and over again that I was sorry. I tried to come up with any excuse I could to calm him down, but he just kept lookin' out the front window and drivin' and drivin' until we reached the cemetery and he told me to get out.

"Please, Junior."

He laid hands on me that night. He beat me in the cemetery. There was no amount of hands I had that I could throw up to protect myself from him. He just kept on and kept on saying "I caught you. I caught you." That's all he said. It was like he had checked out and there was nothing left but rage. I don't like to talk about it.

We drove back home silent but my mind was goin' a mile a minute. I wondered how I would get out. No job. No parents to run to. I wondered how I would make it through. I worried about my children.

And if you wanna know the truth, that's the night I knew for sure that I was trapped. And I been trapped ever since.

So, I come to church just like Ma made us do. He hate me

comin' here. But I guess he figure there ain't no way he can stop me. It's too many women here that care about whether or not I show up. But they all got they own problems. They own men.

I make my children birthday cakes. I make sure they fed and clean and that they get to school. That's what I'm supposed to do. But that man ain't got no wife. All he got is a woman he pour all his crazy into that's dyin' to get away. My oldest boy is long and lanky and good with sports. My girl got a spirit and a passion about life and she stay curious. And my youngest boy, the one up here singin' his heart out right now, I know he won't ever disappoint me. He love his Ma. And he sho' can sing.

The old woman who wouldn't smile at Tuan is standing up to leave. He fixes his big, brown eyes on her again. But this time, he wants nothing from her. He seems to be only fascinated by how old she is.

She first places her cane out into the aisle and uses it to hoist herself up with a great deal of effort and concentration. Tuan is looking from her face to the cane and then back again. I wonder what could be going through his mind. He, of course, does not yet understand that this is how he will end up some day. This is how all of us will end up some day, if we live long enough.

He watches her as she stands up as straight as her body will allow. It isn't very straight at all.

Her enormous purse swings from her forearm like the pendulum of a grandfather clock. I look away out the window. The old woman's condition hits too close to home.

The bus is nearing the spot where one of my favorite bars used to be. Till this day, it is one the grimiest places I ever frequented. But like a lot of the places where I spent my youth, it has been demolished. In the spot where it once stood, someone has planted an array of stunningly colorful flowers. I find this ironic.

The place was where I drank gallons of whiskey and learned about tops, bottoms, rice queens, snow queens, bears, otters, chubby chasers, femmes, butches, twinks, and chicken hawks. The hefty, endless supply of drugs. Where I honed what I thought manhood was supposed to be. That place is gone. Now it's all flowers.

The old woman is walking with great difficulty toward the front of the bus. Someone pulls the cord for her. She passes me and smells exactly how I thought she would. Of floral perfume.

Tuan stares at her openly, with his mouth agape. Maybe he's wondering why she walks so slowly. I want to explain to him that age will catch up with us all. I look out the window again.

I spent too much time at a place that no longer exists. I spent too much time looking for something that I still haven't found.

THIS GAY LIFE

The heavy door of The Holiday always slammed hard behind whomever had just passed through it. This racket would cause the patrons sitting at the bar to look up from their drinks and turn their heads in unison to peer through the darkness, trying to get a peek. You could gauge your attractiveness for the evening by quickly counting, without being obvious, the number of seconds their collective heads hung in the air after the door slammed behind you. Anything less than three seconds would probably have been enough reason for you to turn around and go back home. But one always held out hope that, once that door slammed, your Lancelot would be standing on the right side of it. It would take his eyes a moment to adjust in the darkness, but once they did and locked onto yours, there would be nothing but adventure for the rest of the evening, sexual validation, and pleasure.

The Holiday sat dimly lit between two college campuses. There were no windows. It had the rather astounding ability to appear deserted, even though it was smack dab in the middle of the city. Walking past, you might completely miss that telltale heavy door if you weren't looking for it. In short, it was a dive; a one-room hole in the wall with a horseshoe bar at the center and all varieties of male homosexuals scattered around, anchored fast to barstools or standing around in shadowy corners. The jukebox that churned out high-energy dance music, one of the few sources of light, always seemed to be fighting against the somber mood of the room.

There were regulars. It was smoky. There was a highly graffitied men's room ("Mark gives good head!!!") in the basement pungent with acrid urine but, as far as I can recall, no ladies' room. The Holiday was uncomplicated. Wooden. An old-fashioned pickup joint. No need to get dressed up because nobody could really see what you were wearing anyway. It was a place for man's men. It reeked of desperation and spilt beer and I loved it.

I liked to go by myself late on off nights in the dead of winter, when the freezing wind and snow that pushed me in would slam that telltale door behind me with all its might. The few heads at the bar would look up to assess me, and I would pretend with everything I had not to be drenched in self-consciousness as I casually made my way to a barstool. I regarded it as if I could take it or leave it, knowing full well that there was no place in the world that I'd rather be. The Holiday is gone now. Just like the Arena Health Club. Just like the Pegasus club. And just like the Images bar. All their bricks have long since been hauled off. But, when they were there, I was young and, when I was drunk and high, I felt gorgeous.

But that was a thousand years ago and I'm sitting here tonight three sheets to the wind in a different gay bar in the same city, remarkably different than The Holiday. This bar is all shiny glass, and passersby can look directly inside as though we are all on display in a poofter terrarium. It is charmingly and warmly lit with candles and there's no smoking. The boys all look healthy and are wearing beards this year. They are smartly dressed and slim in dark clothes, a far cry from what was de rigueur in my day. Not a damn "Act Up/ Cry Out" pink triangle T-shirt or Doc Martens boot in sight. These boys are stylish and handsome in a wholly different way. But I am, as I say, three sheets to the wind, munted on Jack Daniel's and cocaine, so my judgment may be off.

They are sipping cocktails served in svelte glassware. They are talking about celebrities that I have never heard of. But it's nice to sit here for a moment, get out of the house and reminisce, allowing the evening to settle all around me quietly, amid the light tinkling of glassware and soft tasteful music. I'm sitting next to a window so clean that I can clearly see all passersby as they look me in the eye, knowing full well that this is a gay bar. I can see them and they can see me seeing them. This is something that you could never do at The Holiday. There, you were swaddled in a cradle of darkness and protected from the world outside by solid brick and oak. Once that telltale door slammed, you entered into another world, a fortress. The banging of that door behind you signaled that all of your worldly problems, all of the straight people, all of the pretending could go away. The sound of that slamming door had the power to transport to another dimension: a safe space of gay men and only gay men just for a few hours. But I'm going to go sit by the window in this place and look passersby right in the eye and dare them to cast me a disapproving look, because I can do that now. I am now normal. I catch the eye of a young man across the bar and I smile. He looks away immediately and begins to fiddle with his cell phone.

Back in the nineties, at The Holiday, the man across from me is staring at my twenty-three-year-old self. It's so dark that I cannot quite make out whether or not he's worth my time. I pretend not to notice, but I can feel him looking. In the days before smartphones, it was difficult to find a place to train your eyes so that you didn't look like you were out "looking." It required skill. You could pretend to be reading the local *Out* magazine, or you could train your gaze down at your drink or the floor, but that was about it.

I can feel the man staring at me. When I look up, he averts his eyes and when he looks up, I avert mine. The pre-coital waltz.

I stand up to subtly give him a full look at what he might literally be about to get into. I yawn and stretch in a spectacularly obvious way to show him that I am fit, with my flat stomach and muscles, before I walk over to the jukebox that has the added benefit of casting a little light on my smooth, young face. I want him to take a look at those goods as well.

I pretend to flip through songs, none of which I'm remotely interested in. I flip and pose. Flip and pose. All the while conscious of his eyes on me. I go downstairs to the bathroom, do a little coke and come back up. I flip and pose and pose and flip until it is time to make my way back to my barstool where there is a free drink waiting for me. "It's from that guy," says the uninterested bartender through the cigarette still pinched between his lips. He has seen this dance millions of times. I grip my free drink in my hand and raise it in a gesture of cheers toward the figure in the corner draped in shadow. He raises his glass too. I cannot see his face, but I can feel him wink.

The young man who has just spurned my smile at this glass-walled, stylish bar is now tending to a drunk girl. I imagine she is his hag. Because this place is built like a sodomy aquarium, she has walked smack-dab into a large floor-to-ceiling window with the full force of her body, thinking that it was a way out, like a dumb goldfish. I can actually see how she made the mistake. The force of her head and body on the window made a loud *thwak,* and not one person has had the balls to even giggle. Instead, a few run to her aid to see if she is okay.

I have no such problem laughing at her loudly and pointing, looking around to see who I can get to join in with me. But people are just looking at me strangely, and my attempts to talk to them are falling on deaf and irritated ears. I may have had too much to drink. All I do is drink. I have lost two jobs and many friends because of it.

In addition, I cannot seem to catch the disapproving and contempt-filled eye of any passersby through this window. They appear not to care that I'm gay and that I'm sitting brazenly in a gay bar with a large picture window so that they can clearly see that I am out and proud. I look around at the young faces and I feel myself disappear under their brief gaze, as they move on to looking at the next man. The younger man. I order another drink. Because why not?

The bartender at The Holiday has placed another free drink in front me, courtesy of the man across the bar. He and I are now two of the few patrons left, when he finally works up the courage to make his way over. He has been sending drink after drink my way, and we are both now fully drunk. He staggers a little into the light of the juke-box and I can see almost immediately that he is not worth my time. He is old. Unprepossessing and plain. He has tried his best to give it the old college try at looking youthful by employing an overdone black leather jacket worn over the standard plaid flannel shirt. He is at least fifty if he's a day. His body is nothing to write home about. He is short and squat, which is a difficult thing to determine when someone is perched on a barstool across the room from you. These are the risks you take. I am not sure if my face made any attempt to disguise my disappointment, but I know that he's not worthy of me and my youth.

I resent him for attempting to lure me in. I am not sure what his attraction to me says about myself, but it can't be anything good. I am wondering when he will make his move when he finally sits himself next to me and tries to continue the pre-coital waltz. He flops himself on to the stool next to me and now I can see that he is flabby. He has let himself go. This will not stand. I begin to scan the bar for whomever might be left. There has to be someone better.

He begins the usual banter, buying me another drink and another drink and I take them all, knowing full well that I have no intention of delivering on the expectations that I can now see reflected in his glassy eyes. My responses to his questions are monosyllabic. With each drink, he moves his barstool closer and closer, and I feel a sense of surprising anger rise up in my chest. He is now pestering me. I don't know why he's even out. I don't know why men like this don't just stay home. I've come all this way and spent all this time talking to him and now he expects me to put out just because he's bought me a few drinks. His hand finally finds the courage to make its way all the way up my thigh and I scoot away violently, causing my own barstool to scrape the floor like a needle snatched off a phonograph record. I have had enough. It is now that, in no uncertain terms, I need to tell him that he has no chance with me. He is not in my league and frankly, I'm offended that he could even think such a thing. It's time to tell him that, although I think he's nice or whatever, this thing just isn't going to happen. The remaining patrons look up at us, drunkenly waiting for the drama to unfold.

This glass bar that I'm sitting in now in the middle of this newly gentrified neighborhood used to be called something else. But I am far too drunk, unsteady, and clumsy to remember what it used to be called. I do remember that my friends and I used to call it the "Wrinkle Bar." The men who tended to frequent this place were old and past their prime. Shouldn't have been out, really. They made our fine young hides feel cheaply superior with their hungry and pitiful stares. And the way that they so nakedly sought after us was pathetic, singular in its desperation.

We made a point of ignoring them so that they knew they were being ignored. We hit the front doors of this place like a hurricane early on a Saturday night before we actually "went out" for real, trying hard to look casually masculine in outfits that we'd taken hours to put together.

We'd make our way to the bar and there the old, pitiful men sat; sallow-skinned, rooted to barstools all in a row like onions, heads hung low, looking deeply into their drinks, as if their glasses were wells in which they'd accidentally dropped their hope. We made sure they noticed us and then we made sure to shame them for doing so. They were jealous because they were too late to take advantage of all this Freedom, we told ourselves. Back then, these huge windows were made primarily of impenetrable opaque glass block. Now it is a conservatory of unapologetic queerness.

The people here have changed, gotten snooty. Dressed up for a bar. Not one of them has accepted my offer of a drink. They have somehow all become younger and have managed to make me feel quite out of place. So I drink more and stare down at my phone and then I stumble to the bathroom occasionally. I try to play some popular music on the jukebox. The machine is a complicated thing that sits up on the wall with endless digital displays of artists I've never heard of. It doesn't even take actual money and I have to dig around in my pocket for a credit card. I swear at the contraption and I drop my credit card a few times before I find a song that I like. When I start to dance, the eyes in the room are all on me. All furrowed brows and pursed lips.

The bearded boys have no interest in me. I tap one on the shoulder as he's walking by to try to get him to dance with me and he jerks away. These boys don't even know. They sip their expensive drinks and glide around the bar, making small talk, and not one of them remembers Act Up/Cry Out or my pink triangle T-shirt that showed that I was conscious. We, us homos from the nineties, are the ones who put in all the real work so these youngins can enjoy all this pellucidity. We are the ones who did all the heavy lifting.

I am going to be asked to leave this bar soon. I am too drunk to be in public. I can see the man I tried to make dance with me making his way over to the manager. He is telling the manager that I'm causing trouble.

"We don't want any trouble," says the bartender at The Holiday. The man who has bravely crossed the bar to see me is in a rage. He has spent a lot of money on me only to be insulted. He has grown belligerent and called me names. He wants his money back. He wants me to apologize. I cannot be bothered with what he wants. The bartender tells him that, if he doesn't calm down, he will be asked to leave, and I take secret pride in the fact that I have brought all this fuss about. Over *me*. Because when you're young, everything is "Me."

The man lowers his voice and apologizes to the bartender and begins to put on that awful leather jacket. When he does, he turns to me and does not meet my eyes. He looks only at the floor as he addresses me. The full atrocity of his age is half-lit by the glow of the jukebox. He speaks in a very measured and calm way. He trembles a little with anger and embarrassment.

"Someday," he says. "Someday you won't look good. You're not always going to be young. Someday everything you're so proud of right now will be gone forever, and I wish that I could be there to see it."

I am amused by his ridiculousness, and I talk shit on him to the bartender after he leaves, humiliated. Sour grapes are never attractive.

By far, the most horrible thing about this glass bar, this cellophane palace in which I currently sit, is the fact that everywhere you turn is a reflective surface. Looking drunkenly out the window, I can see my own face. The alcohol doesn't work to make me feel gorgeous anymore. There is only so much it can do. I am cracked and old. Crow's feet. Worry lines, puffy eyes, turkey neck, and wrinkles; a face caving in on itself. I can't help but notice the fact that my gut has overtaken my belt buckle, bravely shielding it from the elements. The craggy outline of my sour jaw and yellowed and tired eyes. I can't help but see the thinning and rapidly graying hair. It all comes around and around and around and absolutely no one is immune. I have drunk too much tonight and for too many other nights for that matter and it is beyond time for me to make my way home, as I can see that the manager has pretty much had it with my presence. I don't want to go home, so I'll probably head to another bar because I'm fine when I'm around people. It's when I'm alone that the real trouble starts.

Before the manager does me the favor of physically removing me, I gather my black leather jacket and stumble to the door.

Tuan's mother is meeting him and his father downtown after she gets off work. I know this because I have sat this whole bus ride listening to the young father's conversations. I am still listening. Maybe they will go to a department store, he says. Or maybe they will eat at a fast-food restaurant that will give Tuan a kiddie meal with a plastic toy.

Tuan is tugging at the tag inside the neckline of his shirt. He is cranky and getting sleepy.

As I listen in, I am struck by how lonely a family making plans makes me feel. The isolation and disconnection in my own life is near total. It is keeping me safe from my old troubles, but it keeps me apart at the same time. It is the bargain I have made and that maybe I deserve.

I know that I never want to go back to the endless, desperate ache of begging someone to love me. I have been there. I know it like the sound of my own breathing. I know how deceptive a crumb of it can be when I feel starved for it. I want to learn to love myself, as they say. I'm not entirely sure what that even means, but I hear other people say it and it sounds good.

LOOK LEFT, LOOK RIGHT

This one is pulling my pubes. It hurts, like she's stabbing my crotch with tiny needles, but I try not to let it show. This room is too bright, but I stare straight up into the light on the ceiling anyway. Now she's tearing at my pubic hair like she's ripping out errant threads from an old sweater. I shut my eyes tight and let her poke around.

I've gotten good at telling which ones will make it and which ones won't. This one won't. She's afraid of my dick. I could tell she was afraid of it when she walked into the room, before she even saw it, cheeks red as poinsettias and the rest of her face flushed deathly white. Already sweating and nervous. They're supposed to greet me when they walk in, like the doctor's assistants they're training to become. But she breezed past me, head down, and went straight for the rubber gloves. Didn't introduce herself either. Couldn't look me in the eye. You can't be a good physician's assistant and be afraid of dick. I just don't see it happening—also, she's pulling my pubes.

She's sliding inexperienced rubber gloves over my balls as if she doesn't know how sensitive genitals can be. I'd be willing to bet that mine is the first dick she's ever seen.

White walls, white lab coats, white people. I turn my head to the left to read about the symptoms of diabetes. The chart has an overweight, faceless cartoon man on it, and he's holding a hamburger.

The symptoms floating around him are written inside word balloons: shakiness, erratic behavior, sudden weight loss, sexual problems, blurry vision. I wonder if you and I might also have diabetes.

"Find the perineum, Courtney."

The proctor has been patient, trying to let Courtney figure out my penis on her own. She then begins a process of gentle instruction I've heard five times today. That's a total of ten white hands on my dick, all from women. Courtney's new white coat is brilliant. She looks every bit the part, but her nervousness betrays her. Finally, I say to the ceiling flatly, trying to help her out, "Oh, there it is. I feel it."

I cough. Twice. Just to get it over with. Courtney is not going to make it, but she still has to put her finger up my asshole. I know she'll shove it inside so forcefully that I won't be able to help but yelp. Then she'll palpate like she's trying to fish her wedding ring out of a sink drain before she tries to push my prostate out through my throat.

I bend over, rest my elbows on the little table, and spread my legs unprompted. This is always the hardest part, so I try to think of something else. I think of your beautiful brown eyes and how they'll light up when I show them money. Then we'll make the call, and you'll be talkative and convivial like you used to be as we board the bus. You'll sit next to me as we make our way to buy what we need.

Our feast-or-famine attitude toward getting high has to stop, and that's why we're going to ration it better this time. Make it last.

You haven't been yourself lately, but I'm bringing the money to you. Three hundred dollars for one hour's work. That should keep us for a couple of days if we're careful. We weren't careful last time. It's greed that keeps us desperate. I'll clean my apartment, so we can just talk while we get lifted there. I'll wash that rotting pile of dishes in the sink and on the kitchen floor, pick up all the corroded takeout containers, and launder my filthy clothes. This time, I'll put the drugs to good use. We won't just use the high to run around the city looking for more high. I know better now. We'll do it together.

Maybe you'll want to have sex with me again, but I want you to know that's not all I'm looking for.

I found this gig at the university the last time I cleaned my apartment. It was advertised in an old newspaper. All you have to do is swallow your pride for an hour or so and they hand you cold hard cash. I've had so many white women's fingers in my ass today and I don't feel the least bit ashamed. I'm doing my part for medicine, if you really think about it. These girls have to get their education from a live human with a cock, and it may as well be me.

The trick is to not look down. I made that mistake once and looked into the face of a disgusted young damsel with an upcurled lip. She was staring at my penis like it was broccoli she'd been ordered to eat. I can feel them dismissing the myth about Black men as soon as they lay eyes on it, but any man's dick would shrivel up under these conditions. It's best just to not look down, and think about something else as they thrust their skinny digits inside me.

So as Courtney stabs at my anus, I focus on why I need to be here. I'm losing you. You don't smile at me anymore until we get high. Until I buy the medicine to cure your listlessness. My calls go unanswered. I'm forced to visit you late at night.

I go out with no bus fare, which doesn't really matter because the buses have stopped running long before I take to the streets.

I emerge from my house in the wee hours, high as a kite, my mind buzzing with a swarm of wasps. With a nervous feeling in my stomach, I hit the road. It's not a comfortable walk. It's cold. Three miles there and three miles back. I sometimes go back and forth three to four times a night until the sun comes up. Walking to your house, getting too cold waiting outside for you to come home, walking back to my house, then worrying I missed you, and making the trip all over again. The doctor at my last rehab called this "compulsive."

I remember every detail from my solitary walks. I remember the quiet. I remember how I could hear the wind rustling through the trees and the faint sound of car horns from miles away. I remember how cold the autumn air would become. A family of raccoons rifled through trash in the rear parking lot of an apartment building once. My walking would occasionally incite the vocal cords of someone's dog or set off a motion-activated porch light, but my pace was always steady. I ignored my stinging fingertips, numb nose, frozen cheeks, and the damp perspiration under my coat. Streetlight to streetlight along the empty sidewalks, I passed houses where the lights were all out and the people inside were surely nestled next to their lovers.

All this, to get to you.

One night last week, I called you over and over again from a bar downtown. You didn't answer and my phone died. I had really hoped you'd come. I had everything we needed in my pocket. But you never answered, so I did it all myself. I was the last person in the bar and, when the bartender told me I had to go home, I really didn't know where to go. So, I walked to the Liberty Tunnels, which is so narrow and not meant to be walked through, but I went inside anyway. I was high as a kite and cars zipped past me, coming within inches of my body. The drivers leaned on their horns and yelled out their windows, asking over and over again if I was some sort of crazy person. I hoped that one of them would hit me. I closed my eyes tight whenever I heard a car approach me fast from behind. I closed my eyes and waited to be tossed in the air by a bumper. Tossed up to God.

I barely got to the middle of the tunnel when a police car came up behind me flashing its lights. I guess someone called them on me and told them that a crazy man was walking through the narrow tunnel. The policemen yelled at me. I think they could tell that I was high but they didn't want to be bothered. I asked them if they could take me home and they laughed. They just drove me to the other side of the tunnel and left me there. I don't remember much after that. It was embarrassing.

I have come to terms with the fact that I have somehow willingly allowed myself to be emptied out and refilled with devotion to you. The shrink at my last rehab called me "compulsive" and "depressed," but he doesn't understand how much I love you. This is not like all the other times. You're not like all the others. This time, it's for real.

The thought that you might be in your apartment with that other man hollows out my bones.

At the end of your street, I slow down and creep on the balls of my feet. My heart beats out of my chest because I know, even in my current state of mind, you might be unnerved to see me slinking around your house at this hour. Perhaps you'd not want to be my friend any longer. You've told me several times that you don't feel that way about me, that you just want us to "be friends"—until we get high and you express how you truly feel. I know you're seeing someone else, but you are the one who is going to save me. The last one didn't. He said I was "unstable." I know I can save you, too, if you just give me the chance.

I'm glad your cat can't talk. She can see me from her seat in the window. She knows my face. In those iridescent eyes staring down at me, I spot recognition. If she could talk, she would tell you I am outside your home dripping with fealty. I stand there for a long while, ducking the nosy headlights of the occasional passing vehicle. I hope you arrive home from a late night with him so I can stop you both at the doorstep and tell you how I feel. You never arrive home with him. Maybe you're inside. I creep closer to the building and think I see a curtain move, a light come on. I walk to the middle of the street and stand there, looking up. Maybe I should ring the doorbell, but I decide that would be too crazy. It might put you off. I don't want to scare you. I congratulate myself for coming to this conclusion. I am not unstable.

The man you're seeing has lots of money. He owns his own business, I've heard, and he can buy you all the dope you want. And that's why I come here to let women like Courtney ram their index fingers in my ass. Just one night with you is all I want. Five index fingers up my ass. Four to go.

Courtney removes her rubber gloves with two snapping sounds

and basically runs out of the room. No way she's going to make it. I've done this enough times to be able to tell from bedside manner, and she has none.

My asshole feels like it's just been massaged by the business end of a rototiller. The insides of my buttocks are greasy with lube, which makes me feel like I've shit myself. But I always make a point to clean myself well before I come here, out of respect for the students. I cover all my scars for the same reason. I don't want them to think I'm unstable. The proctor gives me a look of concern.

"You ready for the next one?"

I turn on a chipper smile. "Oh, yes! Bring it on!"

I'm shaking and can't tell whether it's because I'm cold or I want to get high. Courtney closes the door behind her and I stare out the window. I wonder what part of the city you might be in. Today is gray, cold, ugly with rain. The white brightness of this room makes the window look like an old black-and-white television. I look out at buildings and over rooftops and imagine how happy you'll be once you know I have what you need. I'm smiling as the door opens once again.

Another trainee enters the room all perky and convivial. She thrusts her hand out. Her cheeks are like begonias. I don't want to shake her hand but I do.

"Hi! My name is Madeline and I'll be performing a hernia check and prostate exam for you today! Is that alright?"

Of course it's alright, Maddie-baby. My name is Brian and I'm a drug addict who needs $300.

"Would you mind lifting up your gown for me?"

She's beaming. Her smile is tense. Forced. She wears perkiness like a suit of armor. She goes down on me to rub her gloved fingers all over my exhausted bumtickler. I close my eyes and dream of redemption.

On Tuesday, I went to your house and no one was there. Instead of going home, I decided to check The Infinity Bar. The one with the big windows. I didn't have any money so I didn't go inside, but

I stood outside and saw you. You looked so beautiful with him, the big shot with his own business. You've never faced me on a barstool like you were facing him. He had your full attention. Your full presence. Your body was fully turned toward him, and you were resting your arm on the bar and your head in your hand as you gazed into his eyes. You were smiling with what looked like love. I could feel it from across the street. My breath came panting and choking its way out. My sternum cracked open. The ache was indescribable: a crust of numbness piled on top of a lithosphere of pain piled on top of an outer core of hopelessness, until a white-hot surge of anger finally broke through like a volcano. My body was yanking open the bar door before my head knew what was happening.

I'm sorry about what happened. I'm sorry about the broken glass and all the shouting. Your new friend, the one with his own business, looked horrified. I only remember flashes. I only remember two sets of arms on either side of me pulling me out the door as I grabbed for you. I remember begging. I'm sorry I begged. I remember the tears, but most of all I remember the look of horror on your face. I remember dragging my feet so the bar staff couldn't easily lift me. I see flashes of aghast patrons. You have to believe me that after I sobered up, I was mortified. I remember hitting the sidewalk after the bum's rush, and I remember being stopped from going back inside. You saw me through the window and your face was contorted in a mask of goodbye forevers. Then you turned to your big shot friend who owns his own business and began what I can only assume to be an explanation of how you didn't know who I was. Just to save face, I imagine. I suppose I understand. I am so sorry.

"Please turn your head and cough."

After I was thrown out, I walked straight to your house. I sat on the steps in the cold for hours. I had some coke for us to share, but I used it all trying to stay warm. After a while, my whole body was violently shivering. You never came home. I tried to force the door open. The cat stared down at me from the window. I haven't slept much since.

By now, you must think I'm really unstable.

"Now, could you turn around and put your elbows on the table and spread your legs?"

I'm going to have three hundred whole dollars soon and we can spend it all. Every dime. I will come looking for you when I'm done here, and I'll come get you no matter where you are in the city. We can save each other. I know you like no one else does.

Madeline has been kind to my ass. Six down, three to go. In about a half hour, I will have a fat envelope of twenty-dollar bills. She tilts her head to the side and smiles her big, cloying smile and sticks her hand out again to thank me. She'll make it. Off to the kind of future I will never know. You're all I have. A wave of nausea has taken me over. I can't wait to get out of here. The proctor looks up at me before she closes the door behind her.

"Ready for the next one?"

"Sure thing."

I stumble a little. A concerned look casts a shadow across her face before she silently closes the door. I walk to the window again. I look out over the building and the rooftops into all that black and white. I look down at the front steps of the building, anticipating the moment when I'm out there in the cool breeze, money in hand, rain on my face. I will look left and then I will look right, before deciding where to begin my search for you.

There is a drunk man on the bus now. He boarded in the Wino district that we locals call Soho, near downtown. He is perhaps only a little older than me, with kinky hair and an unkempt appearance. He is ranting and raving at no one and he smells of the whiskey that I learned to love so much. Everyone else is uncomfortable and ignores him except for Tuan. He is fascinated by the man's loudness, but the look in his eyes shows that he also knows that there is something wrong. He stares the way kids sometimes do.

The drunk man looks down at Tuan, who looks up at the man dreamily and with sleepy eyes. I find that I am holding my breath. Not because I think the man is physically dangerous. I'm holding it because I'm scared the drunk man's sorrow and pain will somehow infect the boy's spirit. From my own experience, I know that there is something going on deeper than the whiskey. There is some pain he is trying to escape. I don't want Tuan to see the way that some men — men like me — deal with their despair. Because despair is an insidious and dangerous thing. I know it well.

I went to rehab thinking that I was there just to "dry out" for a few days. I went because I thought that I needed to "take a break" and learn how to drink and drug like a normal person. It sounds silly to me when I think about it today. I now know that I was there because I needed to be there.

Rehab is where I met my friend Robin. She was a crack addict. A Black woman with wide, alert eyes who wore perfectly and a bit heavy-handededly-applied makeup. Purple and blue on the eyelids, scarlet red on the lips. Robin called me out for being a liar in every group session. She saw right through my respectability act and saw just what I was: a desperate addict trying to excuse his behavior.

As the bus travels through Soho, we pass the corner where I last saw her. It was six months after we had both been released. Springtime. I heard her voice before I saw her. Her laugh was very distinctive. Full of broken glass and cigarette ash.

When I saw her, I couldn't wait to tell her that I had been sober for six whole months. It was affirming to see her out in the real world, in the open air laughing. I rushed toward her before my mind knew what my feet were doing. Walking up on her from behind, I was already picturing in my head how wide her smile would be when she saw me. But as she turned around, her face had new lines embedded in it. The makeup that she once so carefully and proudly applied was nowhere to be found. And the eyes that were once so large with rapt attention to detail were glassy and held in place by half-mast eyelids.

My trajectory had been too fast to stop myself from the approach. By the time I was able to take it all in, I was standing right in her face. She looked up at me, confused and suspicious. "It's Brian." And when she didn't respond, I stood there framing my face with my hands like an idiot, thinking that that would somehow jar her memory. Her mouth hung open and her eyes were vacant. She wasn't there anymore.

After a few seconds, a man came up and stood beside her and grabbed her by the bicep and doubled the wine smell. He looked me dead in my eyes, then down to my shoes and then up again. He asked me who I was. Before I could answer, he dragged Robin off by the arm, pulling her down the street so fast that she stumbled trying to keep up. I watched them until they turned a corner. I should have done something. But I don't know what I should have done.

I remember something that she once said in rehab. "Maybe it's childhood. Maybe if you don't feel like you got no love in childhood, you spend the rest of yo life lookin' for it in grimy places."

I look up at Tuan and his father. Tuan is falling asleep. I wonder if, when he grows up, he will look back on his childhood and believe that he was loved. Because feeling loved by Black parents can be tricky. I never felt loved because I was looking for the wrong clues. I was looking for that love that comes from parents who aren't stressed out all the time and are trying to make a way out of no way.

My mother once told me that, when she was a child in the Jim Crow south, a Black parent showing affection toward their children was a sure-fire way to let white people know what your weakness was.

I look over at Tuan again. He will be asleep soon. He is leaning against his father's torso and fighting it. Looking at this little boy at the start of his life makes me wish I could start my own life over knowing that, yes, I was loved. Just not in ways that I could understand.

CARNIVAL

A trip to Hills Department Store in Warren, Ohio, came around only twice a year. Once, when it was time to go back to school and once again when it was time to replace your pair of shoes. Walking into the store just before the school season started was what I imagine children whose parents had money must have felt like when they were taken to the circus. Or maybe to one of those small fairs that popped up in random parking lots — those fairs that were there one day and gone the next and featured a few spinny rides operated by men with tattoos and criminal backgrounds. Miniature amusement parks that lit up the night with sight and sound and filled the air with a warm pretzel, sugar-baked smell. The ones my family was never able to go to. Money issues. So my brother, sister, and I only ever saw them in passing out the window of our rust-bucket of a Buick on our way to pick my father up from the night shift.

We drove past so fast that I only had a second to look out the window before the calliope music would change, sounding alive and inviting as you drove up. But as you kept going, it would warp into a mocking macabre, and the lights would recede like someone slowly taking away your birthday cake. The laughter would trail off in the distance. I could only catch a glimpse of children running around free of adult supervision with one fist filled with red paper tickets trailing the ground, the other wrapped around stems of soft, purple clouds of cotton candy. The whole place was booth after booth of rigged games, offering the promise of giant stuffed animals that few could ever win. I felt cheated every single time we drove past, with my nose pressed against the window of the back seat until I could see and hear no more. And when it was gone, I would flounce back down on the seat, fold my arms, and poke out my bottom lip. And, in those moments, my mother would look back at me in the rear-view mirror and remind me that it was almost the time of year to go back to Hills.

I didn't know it back then, but my mother was a straight up con woman at the now extinct department store practice of deferment known as "layaway," a system where one would basically placate the Layaway Lady by sliding her just a jingle of money at a time, with a promise to pay the full amount, and then reneging on the whole deal at the last minute when the items you wanted went on sale on the main floor. It's a lost art, hustling the Layaway Lady. But a woman gotta do what a woman gotta do, and my mother somehow slowly chipped away at the Layaway Lady's sanity until she got those prices whittled down to damn near negative numbers. It's hard work bamboozling the Layaway Lady. But for my brother, sister, and me, the trip to Hills was all about fun. It was about the chance to sit on one of the reject carousel horses in front of the store that ate nickels as payment for vibrating us into oblivion for three minutes at a time. Those were the only rides we could afford.

The art of running a shell game on the Layaway Lady at the rear of the store takes concentration. My mother needed all her wits about her and commanded the scene carnival barker style, with all the linguistic fluidity of an auctioneer. She couldn't have her annoying children braying nearby, potentially wrecking the whole hustle. So she would give us each two whole concession stand dollars to stay out of her way.

The concession stand was in the small entry room facing the parking lot at the front of the store where the shopping carts were piled up. This antechamber of Hills Department Store smelled like the emotions of a child. Preadolescent bacchanalia. It was dizzying. It was a roasted peanut, soft pretzel factory wrapped inside a chocolate-covered everything. It was the aroma of popcorn; cold, red Slushee; hot dog jamboree with dusty corners; and waxy yellow buildup on the floors at a time when two dollars could buy you the world.

Right next to the shimmering silver of the shopping carts emblazoned with the red and white Hills logo was everything the children whose parents had money enjoyed at their pop-up parking lot fairs, and that made it all taste so much better. It wasn't just a snack bar. It was the mountaintop.

The crabby, old, white concession lady with the hot pink eye shadow and a face like a catcher's mitt was my Goddess of Giving as I handed her my two dollars reverentially, head bowed, and accepted her synthetic foodthings with a gratitude matched only by those who have received a donated kidney.

I sat down on the diner countertop barstools that faced out to the parking lot and placed my hot peanuts to the left of me, my hot dog to the right, and my cold Slushee in the middle and worked them like an assembly line. Handful of peanuts. Bite of hot dog. Heaping red plastic spoonful of red Slushee. Brain freeze. Repeat. The inside of Hills Department Store was my first barstool and, when I was finished, sticky hands and all, it was time to wander the aisles while my mother worked the Layaway Lady.

The automatic doors may as well have been two gallantly dressed footmen bowing to allow me across the threshold. The glass slid apart and I stepped through into a Wonderland that smelled like *new* things. New leather and new perfume. I was under the Big Top inside every color of the rainbow, having left the smell of food behind to breathe in the pure and potent smell of Capitalism.

Oz. Narnia. Xanadu. *Hills.*

My mission was to lay my sticky fingers on every item on the sales floor and caress it with a child's lust. Wantonly. And I wanted everything. Directly in front of me is the jewelry department and the path to the left will take me to Toyland and, if I wanted a long journey, the lawn and garden department beckoned way over there with its smell of fertilizer and shiny rubber.

The three wholly different directions in which my brother, sister and I would scatter expressly defined our personalities: brother to his dugout of ball, bats, and helmets and sister to her land of dollies and make-believe. I would creep stealthily toward the women's clothing section. I would do so knowing somewhere down deep that it was wrong. It wasn't exactly like I wanted to *wear* girls' clothes. It was just that girls' clothes were so much more interesting. But I knew down deep that it was wrong. I had been told several times by both my parents and I knew especially that my father didn't like it. My parents didn't like a great deal of my behaviors and my father had gripped me by the shoulders on several occasions to tell me plainly and in stern and pointed language while looking directly into my eyes: "Brian. You. Is. A. BOY."

He said it with short stops between each word to give each one time to bore its way into my consciousness. "You. Is. A. BOY." These were the words playing repeatedly in my head as I crossed from the jewelry department to sundries and finally into that place I really wanted to be: Women and Girls. The store smelled different here.

They undoubtedly perfume ladies' clothes before they put them on the rack. This must be some sort of marketing tool because the Ladies' Department smelled of lilacs and vanilla. In stark contrast to the dismal browns and grays of the Men's Department, there was vibrancy, color, and life. There were floral patterns and stripes and ribbons and bows. Even the mannequins were friendlier, posed in inviting ways, and, unlike the mannequins of the Men's section, had heads and faces. Fully made-up faces and posed with arms outstretched in frozen arabesque. They were beautiful dancers petrified in a state of shellacked grace, staring off into the distance. Not one judgment. They wore wigs and shiny beads, downy feathers, and purple tulle. Someone took great care to put their shoes on and the sharp metal spines and Christmas tree bases holding them up were barely noticeable. The music was more resonant here as well. I was being asked if I knew the way to San Jose by a smooth and soulful lady's voice.

I ran my fingers along the clothes hangers, taking in the feel of every fabric imaginable, from rough wool to tenuously delicate silk. This place was a giant replica of my mother's closet, where I would hide some days before baseball practice, hoping I would not be found and drop headfirst into another biweekly cataclysm of unco-ordinated embarrassment. Here were racks and racks of clothing hanging majestically in the style that Miss Diahann Carroll wore on that show where she was a nurse who was constantly surrounded by white people. There, in the ladies' section of Hills Department Store, was the taste, touch, feel, and scent of freedom from the ac-countability and banausic restraints of boyhood. I would have lived there if I could.

Undernourished white people tend to have a hollowness around the eyes that makes the color of those eyes stand out. Greens be-come emerald and browns become hazel. It's shocking, really. The boy I saw lurking near me in the women's section of Hills Depart-ment Store had that hollowed-out look. He was about my age, eight or nine. His hair was dirty and hung limply around his too-thin face in greasy locks. His rat teeth were bucked and yellow and his cheekbones were sunken. White trash in dirty clothes. I had seen this before. White people don't wear poverty nobly and he was the personification of that fact. Skinny as chicken bones and I could tell, even from this distance, that he smelled of rotten egg. But his eyes were spectacular.

Blue. Azure, cerulean, and baby powder blue all at the same time. They were sunken into his skull like someone had tried and failed to bury them and they shone dazzling against skin that was far too pale to have been healthy. The outsides of his eyes were smudged with dark circles as if someone had wiped their muddy boots on them, and his lashes were meters long and thick as paintbrushes. When his eyes met mine, I knew we were to be enemies.

He was rolling the fabric of a shirt slowly between his dirty-fingernailed hands and intermittently holding it against his body. It was the most beautiful shirt that I had ever seen. It looked soft, but not too soft, and had detailed piping on the cuffs of the sleeves as well. It was just a T-shirt, but what a T-shirt it was. I scanned the bin where he'd picked it up for another one, but there was none to be found. He had the only one in his grubby little fingers and, at that moment, I weighed up and assessed everything I'd ever asked my parents for in my life. On balance, it didn't seem to me like I'd ever asked them for much. I calculated my grades in school up until that point, and it seemed to me that I had done pretty well, all things considered. And, as a child who hadn't asked for much in this life, I knew that I deserved that shirt. I couldn't understand why this trash was holding *my shirt*.

There are moments that lay as markers in one's life. Your parents document your first steps and your first words and your first time pooping in the potty and, if my mother were standing by my side at that moment instead of swindling the Layaway Lady, she would have documented this moment in time as *Baby's First Covet*. My mouth had gone dry and my hands went clammy so I wiped them on my jeans. My mother missed *Baby's First Saunter* when I casually strolled up to this Oliver Twist who had the audacity to be fondling my togs, and I stood right beside him as though I were just only passing through. He eyed me with suspicion and fear. Terror, really. He dropped the shirt only halfway back into the bin but kept a hand on it and tried to look nonchalant, like he wasn't standing right in front of the World and Everybody, perusing girls' clothes like the sissy he was. And he was. An unctuous sissy. Soppingly feminine.

His wrists were thin and brittle as tinder, and his clothes hung on him. I could tell he was too poor to afford that shirt, so I just reached out and started aggressively handling it myself, gripping it in my fist. So there the two of us were. Two growing, red-blooded American boys standing in the Ladies' Department, each with one hand on a shirt that God himself had forbade us to wear. I ran the fabric through my fingers, tugging the shirt closer and closer to me and farther and farther away from him. The fabric met my every expectation. The finest synthetic. After I got a feel for that shirt, I looked him straight into his firework-blue eyes and let him know with my best impression of the boys who bullied me every day that I had come to claim what was mine. But, before I could wretch it from his filthy hands . . .

"Joe!!"

The boy's name was apparently Joe. A boy several years older than him was barking at him from the end of the aisle. A boy who had tattoos and a criminal background. A boy who looked like he ran the Tilt-A-Whirl at a pop-up fair. I could tell he was the previous owner of Joe's clothes. He regarded me briefly but malevolently and with the same piercing blue eyes, though harder around the edges than his brother's. His hair was short on top and long in the back. He wasn't happy with where he'd found Joe and I could feel that they'd been in this exact place before. I could tell that, like me, Joe had been given "lessons" on how to be a man. Joe had been roughhoused, Wet Willied, and pants-ed. Like me. I could tell that Joe had racked up hours in his mother's closet avoiding baseball practices and had suffered the humiliations of Tonka Trucks at Christmas sitting under the tree, instead of the disembodied Barbie torso with hair you could really style. I could tell that Joe's brother was just about at the end of his rope with Joe, and I didn't blame him. Joe was an embarrassment. Joe disgusted me. I wanted to fight Joe with all the strength in my body.

His brother's voice caused him to startle like a rabbit and, in an act that I was sure had been repeated over and over in his home, he dropped my shirt like a baseball back into the bin and ran toward his brother, who cuffed him and dragged him away. My shirt lay spread out before me, waiting to adorn the back of its rightful owner. I held it against my body as I walked it quickly to the back of the store. Back to the layaway.

I'd arrived just in time. My mother had the Layaway Lady's eyes spinning in their sockets with confusion and surrender. She'd double-talked and triple-talked her until that woman didn't know whether she was coming or going. My mother had gotten all of her laid-away items down to sale prices and she was busily removing items from their hangers, smiling slyly and pleased with her skills, when I approached breathless. I handed the shirt up to her. I knew well enough not to tell her where I'd found it. The shirt was just boyish enough to pass. That's why I'd wanted it in the first place. The racing stripes and the piping made it just not girly enough to pass for a boy's shirt, and I knew that now was the perfect time to ask my mother, as she was so pleased with herself for bilking the store and high on her savings. I held up my prize triumphantly and my mother gave me a quizzical and annoyed look. She frowned.

"Boy, if you don't put that *pink ass shirt* back where you found it . . ."

That "pink ass shirt" was more of a carnation color, really. It was pink all over and the piping down the sleeves and around the neck and cuffs was a deep red the color of dried blood. I thought I could fool her. But the pink betrayed me. Color had again betrayed me.

She looked at me with a mixture of disdain and surprise at my boldness. She looked at me like she'd never met me before, like she was seeing me for the first time. She looked at me as though, with the presentation of this shirt, I had gotten beyond her reach and that no scolding or punishment for my strange behavior was ever going to work again. It was as if I'd plunged one of those clothes hangers directly into her heart and I swear I saw tears bubble up and occlude her eyes. Her voice shook a little.

"Brian, that is a *girl's* shirt."

"But nobody can tell. You can't tell. It looks like it *could* be a boy's shirt. Just look at it. Please, can I have it? Please. I won't ask for anything ever again. Please can I have it?"

And from that day to this one, no one has ever looked at me like my mother did that day. It was pity mixed with worry for what was to come. It was the piping-pink manifestation of all she had ever suspected. It was every ball and Tonka Truck they'd handed me for Christmas going dusty and unused in the corners around our house. Writ large and crystal clear, she understood my tendency to sneak into my sister's room to play with her disembodied Barbie torso. And it made evident to her why I tended to notice the colors of people's eyes, instead of the strength of their throwing arms, and was forever enamored with all things "pretty." She looked at me with a concern that no one will ever show me again in this lifetime.

My mother hugged herself around the shoulders and tilted her head back as far as it would go. She took a deep breath before exhaling slowly and I knew it was over when she snatched the shirt from my hands. I froze in shame, knowing that the dream was over. My head lowered on its own, ready for her to throw my shirt disgustedly at the already confused Layaway Lady and snap at her to put this *pink ass shirt* back where it came from. I knew that when we got home, I would pay, just like I paid on the baseball diamonds and basketball courts of the world. My mother would lay away my shame, making the payments last for years and years.

But no, she just put it in the cart.

She exhaled slowly and just let something go. I can only guess at what it was. She just let it go in that breath and threw the shirt in the cart, where it glowed brightly, showing up the dull blue jeans and black T-shirts, gray slacks, and boy clothes. She bought me a girl's shirt, rising up against so much that she thought she'd stood for. She bought it and I wore it.

When I wore the shirt out of the house, I remember my mother really looking at me. Recognizing me. Knowing me. She said nothing. I can only imagine what must have been going on in her head. I wore the shirt only twice to school. The teasing became too much. Eventually, the shirt just disappeared. But my mother, in her own way, stood up for me every time I wore it.

Hills Department Store is gone. But I remember wandering the aisles of the poor kid's carnival looking for myself. I even remember Joe. I feel bad for taking his shirt from him. Joe and I had more in common than I, even then, could stomach. Poor and queer. I hated him in that way we sometimes learn early to hate ourselves when we're different.

I wish I could find him and apologize for hating him so much and for stealing his shirt. I wish I could send my apologies up into the night air and have it reach him through the skyscrapers of the big city I hope he moved to. Wherever he is, he'll sit straight up in bed, waking his husband, who will ask him what's the matter.

"Nothing," he'll say, smiling for a reason he doesn't understand. "I just thought I felt something move."

As the bus begins to close in on downtown Pittsburgh, I feel my anxiety begin to push back against my meds. I close my eyes and breathe deeply like my therapist tells me to do. She tells me that I am the only Black male client she has ever had. This does not surprise me. I sit up straight in my seat and take a deep breath. The first time my therapist asked me to do that, she told me to go to my "safe place." I giggled because this is the kind of liberal psychobabble that I used to laugh at.

I used to think bars were safe places. The bus is passing all of the ones that I used to frequent. They are on one street right next to each other. Their entryways go by in slow motion. The 941 Saloon, the Images Bar, the There Ultra Lounge, Pegasus, The Tilden. All places in which I've made a desperate fool of myself. All places I've been thrown out of and barred from.

I snap out of my montage of shame to look up at Tuan. He is sitting still, of his own accord. His blinks are slow. He's nearly asleep. His father is now talking to another man on the bus that he knows, and when the conversation turns to Tuan, his father looks down at him and notices that the boy has crossed his legs one over the other on the bus seat. Tuan's father reaches down without skipping a beat and uncrosses the boy's legs so that they are splayed and wide open. He wants to break the boy of this habit early. He will do the same if the boy begins to use his hands too much when he talks or if, heaven forbid, one hand finds its way to his hip. The masculine requirements of the body are as endless as they are restrictive.

Tuan then dozes off. Immediately. Like someone unplugged him from a wall socket. His head is lolled over to the side and, for him, everything on this bus has completely disappeared. Even himself. He has no idea that right now, he's sitting like a proper man.

Tuan's father pulls the cord for the bus to stop and stands. I sit up straight in my seat. He lifts the boy's limp body and places the child's head on his shoulder, causing the boy to twitch but not wake up. I don't want them to leave.

Tuan's father grabs his bag and informs the driver that he wants the next stop and jumps in the air a little to readjust the boy's position on his chest. I wonder if my father ever carried me in this way. I'm doubtful. Any care for children — even carrying their sleepy bodies — he deemed "women's work." He was steadfast in his beliefs about how boys and men should behave.

When I was little, I sometimes crept into my sister's room to play. Her room was small with just enough room for her bed, a small closet, and a tiny trunk that was filled with her old toys. I liked her toys better than mine. They were colorful and demanded a level of creativity that the clunky trucks and balls I was always given did not. Her dolls asked that you provide them with a personality, a backstory, and a wardrobe, while trucks just sat there looking up at you dumbly. They were little more than hunks of plastic with wheels. They did not spark my imagination nor did they make me curious, but my sister's toys were a place where I could get lost in worlds of my own creation.

When I slowly opened up her toy chest, her dolls looked up at me wide-eyed and expectant. At a certain point in her girlhood, my sister had abandoned them. She had taken to throwing shoes on top of them, which left their hair in complete disarray and their clothes disheveled and indecent. I took them out one by one and set them on the floor. I made sure to keep an ear out for noises in the house. I had given them all names.

"Hello, Miss Melissa."

"Good afternoon, Miss Lynette."

Miss Lynette was a debutante who was trying to find her way in the world without making use of her father's vast fortune. Things were especially difficult for her, as she was just a bust. She was the head and neck of a white girl with long, blonde hair, big blue eyes, and an empty look. The area where her shoulders should have been was fashioned like a tray, a pink tray where you could lay her cosmetics and combs while you worked on her face. Miss Lynette's hair would become longer if you pulled it at the ponytail. But in a fit of rage, my sister had cut her hair preternaturally short, which just added to the list of Miss Lynette's problems.

I would sit her on my lap and ask her questions about her day and what her plans were for the evening. Her plans were always with Steve, a busted-up Stretch Armstrong that I got for Christmas one year and my sister stole. No matter what Miss Lynette did, she could not make Steve do right. She would complain to me as I combed her hair.

Miss Lynette and Miss Melissa did not get along, which was, of course, because of Steve. They both wanted him. And, as things often do with beautiful women and available men, things became messy and Miss Lynette and Miss Melissa were often at each other's throats. Miss Melissa had a deeper voice and a far more stolid nature than Miss Lynette, who was prone to shrillness and theatrics.

"Steve is mine."

"No! Steve is mine!"

"He likes me because I'm prettier."

"You look like a old throwed-away heffa!"

I did their voices as I did their makeovers. I really had no opinion on the subject of who was prettier. I just hoped they'd work it out someday.

The blow to my head came from behind.

It knocked me from a sitting position onto my side and the top of my head collided with the toy chest. For a split second, I thought something had fallen from the ceiling and when I looked up, clothes that were arranged haphazardly on top of my sister's closet fell straight down into my face and by the time I got them off of me, my father's hulking form was blocking the light.

I looked to my left and Miss Lynette was lying on her side staring at me impassively. My father caught me looking to her for help and landed another blow on top of my head. I tried to use my hand to sit up, but he mistook this action to be me reaching for the doll head and hit me again.

"Reach for it again!" He regarded the doll as if it were a weapon.

I stared up at him. I had no intention of reaching for it the first time. But he was daring me.

"Reach for it again!" he repeated.

I backed up and toys from inside the dresser rattled. I'd pushed it up against the window and the curtains fell around me.

"Reach for it again and I will send you back up to God!" he said. "I will send you back up to God!"

I was so ashamed, that I wanted him to. I didn't want to live anymore. It's the first time I recall feeling this way. I wondered if God would take me in my condition. I convinced myself he wouldn't.

I tried to disappear into the wall. I looked up at my father and his eyes had gone black with hatred. His fist was clenched solid as granite, ready to strike again. I went fetal and waited.

"You is a boy!" he said with finality and thunder in his voice.

The next thing I heard was my mother clamoring into the room. I peeked from behind my fingers and saw her pulling at him by the elbow of his upraised arm.

"Just leave the boy alone," she pleaded. "Just leave him alone."

"He can't be actin' like this!" he shouted. "He gonna end up just like Clint!"

Before I was born, my father's youngest brother, Clint, was found dead by hanging in Michigan. Like me, Clint had tried to escape to another place. He didn't get very far nor did his freedom last very long. My family rarely spoke of him and, when they did, they only spoke in whispers. He came up in conversation from time to time only because of the old people — my great aunts and uncles who told my mother that, even more than my father, I was the spitting image of Clint. There are no photos of him to verify this claim. He was found only weeks after his escape from Ohio, and the only thing that anyone would say about him as a person was that he was "different."

My uncle Clint's death was barely investigated. The police determined it to be a suicide, even though Clint's hands were bound behind his back. This fact stayed embedded in my father's skin like a tick. The question of how a suicidal person could tie their own hands behind their back gnawed away at him. He believed in his heart that it was white people who killed his brother. And, as he told me many times, he would rather kill me himself than watch white people do it.

Back in my sister's bedroom, my mother pleaded with my father the way that mothers do. She said his name over and over again, speaking in the gentlest way possible to try to calm him. Her whole body was engaged with the act of pulling him away. She hung from his bicep, leaning back on her heels.

"Just please leave the boy alone!"

My father lowered his fist without taking his eyes off me. When it reached his side, he stormed out of the room, leaving my mother there looking down at me. She regarded me for a moment. Then she cast her eyes toward Miss Lynette who still looked as though she was only there waiting for a train. She stared at the doll for what felt like a long time. She would not look at me.

"Boy, clean this mess up."

Then she walked out.

Tuan's father is not so different from my father. I know now that their actions are not simply from ego. They are afraid, and fear often trumps judgment. It isn't as if they don't have reasons in America to be afraid for their Black children.

WE DIE SOON

GRAVEL

There have been moments of solitude and silence when I have literally taken my right hand, placed it over my left shoulder, and patted myself on the back for surviving small-town Ohio. And if you are a Black person from small-town Ohio, you deserve it too. Go ahead. Do it now. Pat yourself on the back and be proud that you are still standing upright. Because, I may be biased, but I am fully confident that the entire state of Ohio is nothing but a racist cesspool. It wears on the Black psyche until you either leave it forever or get damn good at football. I chose the former.

Just to make sure I made the right decision, I consulted the murky depths of the Magic 8-Ball I've had in my possession since sixth grade.

I asked it if it was a good idea to leave Ohio for Pittsburgh.

Its answer: "Yes. Definitely."

Of course, I didn't know that I was living on the lip of a racist hellmouth when I was growing up. As a kid, my immediate surroundings were my whole world. The only evidence I had that things could be different was what I saw on television. That's how I learned that big cities are often sanctuaries for Black people and gay people. TV planted the seed that I could escape to a better place. Pittsburgh was that place.

The small-minded, racist white attitudes I was leaving behind became more obvious when I put the Buckeye State deep into my rearview mirror. I remember the YOU ARE NOW LEAVING OHIO sign becoming smaller and smaller as the ENTERING PENNSYLVANIA sign became larger and larger.

On Route 76, Pittsburgh entered the frame of the car's windshield gleaming on the horizon like a birthday present, like the Emerald City with the sun glinting off of it. Its beauty from that distance made me silently vow never to return to Ohio, seemingly the long-lost child of Jim Crow, for any reason. In Pittsburgh there was potential for me. That was a first.

When I moved, I reveled in my newfound freedom and basked in the city's broadmindedness. I made friends of all races and backgrounds. It felt like a world away from Ohio, despite the relatively close proximity. It is my home now. Every winter, I wonder why I didn't go someplace warmer, but I like it here.

Even so, Pittsburgh is in America and thus, it has slowly revealed itself to be not as different from my hometown as I hoped.

When I was fourteen, I disobeyed my mother and left the house while she was at work. It was summertime, just after school let out, and all things felt possible. We lived just outside the small, basically rural city of Newton Falls, Ohio, and I wanted to go into "town." I set off walking and forgetting the fact that, even when I was in Newton Falls with my mother, she never let me out of her sight. There were rural roads leading into the city limits and no sidewalks. I did not calculate for this. I took off on foot the way you do when you think you're a grown-up, certain that nothing in this world can harm you. I don't remember what I was going to Newton Falls for. But I do remember that I felt it was the most important thing that had ever been up to that point in history, and my mother just didn't "get it."

It was a road that my mother had driven me down several times on our way to the Sparkle Market to buy our groceries. I had never walked it. It seemed vastly different on foot: unrecognizable, spooky, dark green, and ominous. While walking, cars whipped by me so fast that I hugged the side of the road and took shelter in the grass. Whenever I would hear a car approaching from behind, every muscle in my body would tense and try to make itself narrower. I was helplessly exposed.

And then, I heard the slow crunching of rocks beneath tires behind me.

Not the scattering of them under the wheels of a car that was driving sixty miles an hour, but the slow crunch of gravel, signaling that the vehicle behind me was slowing down. I hoped that it was someone I knew. Maybe one of my mother's friends who would scold me and then force me into the car with the promise to tell my mother what happened immediately. I prayed for this. I prayed for my mother's punishment.

But like so many of my prayers, this one went unanswered.

My first friends in Pittsburgh were Tom, a white, red-headed, and muscular fireplug of a dude; Melinda, a white brunette with cat-eye glasses and a feminist's anger; and Annette, the fearless, tiny, Black lesbian with a shaved head and a progressive attitude toward sex who shepherded me through my first Pride parade. We were liberals in the city, and everything felt alive for us. We loved to go out like you do in your twenties, and we had managed to become part of "the scene." I met people with pet rats and learned how to get high at nightclubs and order martinis. We wore leather pants and danced until dawn. This was nothing like my sleepy life back home. This was the kind of urban existence that I had dreamed of. The whole city was like a jukebox and there was endless freedom to do what I wanted. There was no mother here to tell me that I'd better not leave the house. My friends and I were the very definition of cosmopolitan. To us, there were clubs, hip coffee shops, and cabs as far as the eye could see. I loved it.

One night, we were headed out bar hopping. The hustle and bustle of downtown on Saturday night was all around us, with people laying on horns and shouting at one another. I looked good. I had done my best to tie a necktie in a way that I have since learned is dead wrong. It hung around my neck like a noose. Melinda wore her usual ensemble of all black and clunky military boots. Tom wore denim bib overalls with no shirt underneath. Annette had gone all out. She wore a giant Afro wig, big hoop earrings, white patent leather go-go boots, enormous false eyelashes, ruby red lips, and a half shirt decorated with roses. "Femming it up," she called it.

We were gorgeous.

The gravel crunching under tires had given way to a human voice —a man's voice. He trailed behind me slowly, chastising me for being what he called in the middle of the road.

"Monkeeeeeeee!" he yelled. "Hey, monkey! What the fuck you doin' out here, monkey? You almost made me wreck! Hey! Nigger! You hear me?"

Your body goes clammy all over when you're confronted by an outright racist. Your skin feels heavy and numb at the same time. You shut down, but you can feel the rage you're trying to suppress, boiling like a hot cauldron deep inside. Your stomach becomes a black hole that you wish you could disappear into. The sweat bursts out of every pore on your body.

But something told me not to run.

Something in my Black DNA told me that running would only make things worse. But I remained silent. Something told me to bite my tongue because I was alone and there is no doubt in my mind that the driver saw no humanity in me and would suffer no moral conflict in killing me and dumping my body into the Mahoning River. The man's voice behind me continued to taunt. Only he wasn't talking to me.

There was someone else in the car.

Tom remembered that he needed cash. We ducked into a side street to an out-of-the-way ATM and watched Tom pat himself down for his debit card. He knew he'd brought it but couldn't remember in which pocket he'd tucked it away, so we stood there lined up: Him at the cash machine, frantically patting his own body down, Melinda behind him having decided that she could use some extra cash too, and me and Annette standing behind them on the sidewalk. We chuckled at Tom. We chuckled and never once thought how this arrangement might look to someone on the outside.

Then Tom started to look a little panicked. He became frantic and thought that maybe he'd left his card on the bus. The rest of us were becoming impatient. We were eager to get to the bar and all breathed a sigh of relief when he finally found the card tucked inside his boot. The city was electric with noise as we stood there, waiting for him to insert the card, key in his pin number, and snatch out his drinking papers for the evening. Even though there was noise all around, I could hear the distinctive sounds of tires slowing down behind me. I knew that sound better than I know the taste of the inside of my mouth.

Just outside Newton Falls, Ohio, the driver in the car behind me was narrating our encounter to his passenger, like a tour guide on a safari.

"Look at this nigger taking up the entire road. I should just run him over. I don't know why he didn't just steal a car!"

He laughed loudly. His passenger said nothing. I heard the vehicle pulling around to my side and my blood turned to ice water and my head felt dizzy with static. I wished I'd never left home. I wished I'd listened to my mother. I wondered how cold the Mahoning River was that time of year. I thought to myself that I should at least get a glance at my murderer.

I looked up and he was sneer-grinning at me with pure malevolence in his eyes. Blond hair and yellow teeth. He was driving a pickup truck.

He silently mouthed the word "nigger" and showed me his middle finger. Just over his shoulder, I could see not one but two passengers. Two little towheaded girls with big blue eyes, both in the front seat. They look confused by the driver's behavior, but they'd soon learn what he was trying to teach them. They stared at me with their mouths hanging open, as if they were looking at an animal in the wild.

I locked eyes with both girls before the driver yelled, "Fuck you! Stay out of the road!" and sped off, leaving me in a spray of rocks and dust.

I didn't realize I had been holding my breath until then. I took a big, deep breath and then I wept.

"Hey! Leave them alone!"

Nobody on Seventh Avenue noticed the driver initially, but I heard his tires from two blocks away. "Leave them alone!" the man shouted again, louder this time. I looked at him with bewilderment and, as he kept shouting, Annette noticed him too. He was hollering at the two of us and pointing his finger. We craned our necks toward him, trying to make out what the problem could be. He was in a four-door sedan on his own. A royal blue color that shined like new money.

"I said leave them alone! Leave them alone!!"

Tom and Melinda still did not notice.

The man's shouts were blending into the street noise for them.

But Annette and I were fully alert by then, and had a familiar feeling inching up our spines.

There are moments in life when your situation becomes clear. I imagine there's a moment of realization for people who are drowning, just before they start to kick, flail, and panic. There's a calm inside that is disrupted when your entire system begins to realize that everything is not going to be alright. There are moments like this when something real and consequential happens and awakens something real and consequential within you.

This man had been watching us from his spot in traffic. He had seen two white people and two Black people approach an ATM, and he had seen the white man frantically patting himself down for money. He then saw two Black people: one in a mis-tied tie and the other in a giant Afro wig. The one with a bad tie has his hand tucked firmly in his pocket.

This driver assumed that a nice white couple was being held up by two animals. He assumed the responsibility of hero. He would save the day by calling attention to our crime. He was shouting loudly enough that people on the street turned to look at Annette and me. He was pointing an accusatory finger from the safety of his vehicle. We were urban crime personified. He had seen it on the nightly news, no doubt: how predatory Black people were holding up whites at ATMs across Pittsburgh. He was doing a good thing.

When it became clear to me what the driver was doing, a rage built up within me. But it was the wrong kind of rage. It was the kind of Black rage, wherein you need white people to validate you. I spat at him words to that effect.

"These are our friends! We are *with them!*"

I regret these words to this very day.

They were spoken by a manboy who never learned that he doesn't need white people to prove anything to anyone or to validate his existence. I used Tom and Melinda as a shield, a glowing white shield against the dismissal of my humanity.

I have gone over what I should have said in my mind a thousand times. I should have just told him to go to hell, to mind his own business, to fuck right off. But I chose to have Tom and Melinda's whiteness take the place of my self-respect.

Ohio had taught me well.

When Tom and Melinda finally noticed what was happening, they did nothing. They said nothing. I imagine this kind of thing had never happened to them before. But Annette and I unloaded on the driver for every time we'd been followed around in a store, for every time we had been falsely accused, for every time we'd been dehumanized.

When the man in the car realized he'd made a mistake, he offered no apology. Just a middle finger as a defense against Annette's cursing and my incoherent shouting.

I thought I had escaped by moving to a real city, but I know better now.

When I look around Pittsburgh—the city in which I still live, the city I love—I see a bigger version of what I'd thought I left back in Ohio. A shinier, busier version. A version that has a Civic Light Opera and all-night diners and beautiful museums. But there is no substantive difference. And I have given up on the idea that there is any place in this country that would be any different.

Tuan and his father get off the bus at Smithfield Street and I watch them as they get smaller and smaller, making their way down the sidewalk. Tuan is bobbing like a rag doll in his father's steady grip. The bag slung over the father's shoulder contains only boy toys.

I unzip the outside pocket on my suitcase to make sure that I have my copy of James Baldwin's *The Fire Next Time.* I found Brother James when I was a teenager and it comforted me to know that, at some point, there was a man like me out there in the world who seemed to have found his way. When the Internet came around, I watched old interviews with him wherein he gave off a powerful presence and I dreamed that I could be like him someday. I am no James Baldwin, but I want to start trying to be more like he was: confident and strong and unafraid. So I am leaving this American soil for the first time in my life. I am going alone and I am terrified.

I check the pocket on my suitcase that contains my little helpers. One for depression. One for anxiety. I think about my father, and the clarity that comes with age tells me that he must have suffered from these conditions as well. He was anxious. He was lonely. And he was insecure. There is no thing on earth more dangerous than a man who refuses to accept that he is carrying all of these loads, because it then becomes up to everyone else to carry them for him in one way or another. Other people have to pay the price for his insecurities. If my father could not be the "man of the house," he didn't seem to want to be anything at all.

After the incident with Miss Lynette in my sister's bedroom, I did not cry. Each time I felt a sob rise to the surface, I would choke it back down. I suspect that this was when my initiation into Black manhood really began. I placed a pillow over the face of bad feelings and held it there until they stopped moving, until I was sure that they were dead. But they never really die. They just find other ways to escape. I am learning to sit with them now.

After I cleaned up my sister's room as my mother told me to do, I went out to the back stoop to wait for my father to appear with candy and soft words, but he never came. He never offered those words to me again after that. I sat on the back stoop waiting for him until the sun went down and my mother called me in for dinner.

There are times now when I imagine myself as an adult sitting there wrapped up in shame and hurt and he comes out and places his large hand on my back and tries to dam up the river with bricks.

"Stop cryin' now."

"No."

"You done cried enough now."

"I haven't cried nearly enough."

Then I let go with everything I have, burying my face in my hands. I let my slobber and snot fly. I squeeze my eyes shut tight in an attempt to drain myself of every single tear. And when I have exhausted every muscle in my body with the act of expulsion, I look up and turn to him.

He is not there.

STALL

"Y ou go on in there and *talk* to yo Daddy."

My mother is whispering but emphasizes the word "talk" with a squeeze of my hand as if she thinks some sort of deep revelation between my father and I will break a levee between us, setting free a long-ago dammed-up river of love. I've come back to Ohio and am standing in the nursing home where my father lies dying in bed just down the hall. I don't even want to be here to tell you the truth. I feel little to no connection with the man lying in that bed down the hall. My mother seems to want an emotional scene, the kind that my family has always avoided, so I don't understand these theatrics. I don't know why she's called me here, dropped me in the middle of a soap opera hospital set and commanded me to be an actor. I have no thespian training and I have no emotions from which to draw. The man lying in that room in that bed down this hallway sparks no emotion within me whatsoever.

My mother has been calling me for days, asking me to come here, leaving messages on my answering machine. "Brian, I would like you to come see your father," which evolved into "Brian, you need to come see your father," which mutated into "Brian, you *really have to* come see your father." It is the "really have to" that brings me here because even though I feel nothing for the man, I don't want people to know that I feel nothing for him. So I boarded a Greyhound and left the city to come back to this place. I will miss all the fun of the weekend back in Pittsburgh where my real family and I go out to drink and dance until the late hours. I will call them frequently while I am here in this dying town, where I will be cast in the role of Grieving Son to a man who was cast in the role of Dying Father. My mother is still squeezing my hand and looking at me with an intensity in her eyes, nudging me in the direction of his room. I am confused because she didn't like him much either, but we have to make a show of it, I guess. "You go on in there and *talk* to him," she says again. I play along and start to walk slowly down the hallway toward his room. I wish I were at the club right now where my friends are.

"So, is he like, gonna *die,* or whatever?"

Annette and I are locked in a bathroom stall together at Metropol. She is slowly arching her neck from being bent over a small mirror she's placed on the tank of the toilet seat on which she sits backwards. With one finger pressed down plugging her nostril, she inhales deeply so as not to risk spilling any valuable cocaine. The music outside the ladies' room is nice and loud and we can feel the vibrations even inside our obvious hidey-hole. It gets louder for a few seconds at a time whenever someone opens the door. Annette and I don't whisper. We don't need to because every woman in the bathroom has brought her gay inside a toilet stall to do the same thing we're doing.

"So? Is he?" she repeats when she comes up for air.

"I guess. I don't know. It looks that way."

I take the vial of cocaine from her hand and dig around in my pocket for my tiny spoon.

"Damn. That's deep," she says as she tilts her head back to check her nostrils in the same mirror for traces of errant blow. I admire this ingenuity. "I'm sorry," she adds. "That sucks."

I find my tiny spoon and dig it deep into the cocaine vial in order to get a heaping helping, then maneuver it carefully toward my nostril and suck up a big blast that makes me cough. "It's not a big deal," I tell her. The coke is good. I can immediately feel the synthetic taste of it sliding down the back of my throat and numbing my whole mouth. My ears tingle and my jaw is already clenching. I take another large blast and Annette extends her palm. A sign that I need to hand the vial back. She is ready for another. She has laid the tiny mirror out again and is tending to the business of using her bus pass to chop it up into a fine powder to rid it of its rocks. I like to snort the rocks whole and let them dissolve inside me.

"What, was he, like, *abusive* or something?" she says, not looking up.

The cocaine is so good that I'm feeling loose and communicative. The music out in the club begins to thump louder in my ears and my mouth is already beginning to go dry and I am giving in to the high. With my back teeth already beginning to grind, I tell her that my father was not abusive. He was just a Black father and he behaved like Black fathers are supposed to behave.

"What the hell does that mean?" she asks.

This cocaine is probably the best I've ever had. I close my eyes and lean back against the bathroom stall as Annette starts to cut up another line. I let it work its magic on my tongue and I tell her everything I know.

"I mean, I don't really know him. He used to be part of the family and then he just wasn't. My father didn't want me. He wanted an action figure. I was never boy enough for him. His favorite story to tell is when his own father knocked him unconscious. Can you believe that?"

I look to Annette to wait for a reaction. She gives none. I continue.

"He was unconscious for three days because he talked back to his father. 'He knocked me clean across the room!' My father tells this story like it's funny. He said his father told him that it was better for a Black man to beat his son to death than for a white man to kill him. He said he would never let a white man get his hands on his kids. He'd kill them himself first. Toughen 'em up for whitey. And my father doesn't like women. He once told me that a man's place is over a woman. Head of the household. He used religion to justify it. 'That's the way God intended it,' he said. He told me that women shouldn't wear pants. Can you believe that? He actually believes that women shouldn't wear pants and he believes that if a man wasn't dominating something, then he isn't a man, so obviously I am a huge disappointment. He has to know I'm a fag. I mean he just has to. But he doesn't want to see me. And he likes my brother better. My brother who don't even look like him like I do. Because my brother played basketball and football and ran track and had a ton of girls hanging off his dick all the time. That's what a man is to my father."

Again, I look to Annette for a reaction. Still nothing. This is a good high. I keep going.

"He wrapped everything up in being a 'man' and when he lost his job, he just stopped being anything. He faded into the wood paneling. He doesn't have more than a sixth-grade education, so he couldn't get another job. The steel mill laid him off and then all he did was lay around the house and complain about women and white people."

I can't stop talking and Annette isn't trying to stop me.

"He told me that a Black man has to be ready to fight always. White people gonna test him. A Black man has to control his woman always. Women gonna test him. And when it became clear that I was gonna do neither, he didn't want anything to do with me. And now I'm supposed to go running to this bedside and cry some ol' crocodile tears for a man who chose being a man over just being a father, a human being, a person? So, yeah, I don't know him and I think it's a little too late to try to get to know him now. My mother is acting like we were best friends. Can you believe that? I mean, can you believe it?"

Annette dramatically inhales another line, sniffing more loudly

than necessary and tilting her head back too far. She begins searching through her backpack for a cigarette, the lighting of which will
announce that we're done in the ladies' room for now. She shrugs.

"I don't know, Brian. It could be worse. My daddy was a drunk.
Black men have it hard. But you should definitely go see him. You
wouldn't be here without him and that's gotta be worth something."

She hands me the vial of coke as she is rifling through her bag,
and I quickly scoop up more than my fair share and snort it down
before she looks back up. I hand it back to her and ignore her last
statement. The drugs now have my head spinning. I continue talking, my mouth still motorized by narcotics.

"After my mother left him he didn't know what to do couldn't
even feed himself or keep himself clean he moved into an abandoned house can you believe that my father moved into an abandoned house that was falling down all around him and had no heat
and no electricity just up the road from my house he lived there by
himself with a pile of dirty clothes and a kerosene heater my mother
would send us up there to take him food and make sure that he was
alright but she would never go herself. she would never go herself.
he was an embarrassment he didn't even try after he got laid off
and I didn't know what to do for him I was just a kid but I knew he
was an embarrassment but even then even when he was basically a
hobo he kept telling me to take my hand off my hip act like a man
stop being a sissy he's only sick now because he gave up won't take
his medicine won't eat right won't do anything except sit around and
complain about white folks and women and he just never even tried
he gave up so why should I have to put in any effort at all besides
I'm not even the son he wanted he wanted my brother who doesn't
even look like him like I do and—"

Annette cuts me off. "So don't go then."

I sniff. She lights the cigarette and drops that vial of good coke
into the depths of her backpack. I watch it disappear and suppress
the urge to tell her I want more. She stands quickly and flips the
lock on the toilet stall and we head out to look into the large mir-

ror at the sinks together. We stand next to each other checking our nostrils and she pats down her Afro wig to ensure that the shape is perfectly circular. She reapplies lipstick, rubs her lips together, and then makes kissy faces in the mirror.

"Go see your father. It may be the last time."

We head out the bathroom door and into the hallway that leads to the club where the music is almost deafening and the people are dancing and the flashing lights in the darkness wait to envelop and distract me.

"You want a drink?" Annette asks me.

"Hell yes."

Together we walk down the hallway toward all the things that make life worth living.

I take three steps down the hallway and look back at my mother. I hope to catch her eye, but she is looking at the ground, her fingers interlaced, her lips moving silently, talking to her beloved Jesus, another man from whom I have never felt any emotion. I walk to the doorway where I can see my father lying in the last bed he'll ever occupy. I linger outside for a few seconds until the director yells "Action!" and then I approach my costar. His makeup artist has done an excellent job.

My father is now a dried-apple doll. And while he's never been a big man, he is even slighter in the wake of illness. The sheets that cover his body don't have much work to do. I can make out a bump beneath them that is probably his knee. Larger bumps at the foot of the bed. His brittle arms have been placed on top of the sheets and the hand that once loomed large over my childhood lies limply. His head is turned toward me. The skin on his face has collapsed, exhausted, against his skull, which leaves his eyes wide and searching like a newborn's. His lips move soundlessly. I can't tell if he sees me. I have no indication that he knows that I'm here. I can feel the director and the crew anxiously awaiting me to deliver my first line but I haven't read the script.

You go on in there and talk to yo Daddy.

"I have a fish tank," I say. "In my apartment. There's only two fish in it right now because they keep dying on me."

His wide bloodshot eyes are locked on mine and his mouth moves wetly. Maybe he's trying to say something and it's now obvious to me that he cannot talk. The camera pans back to me. I haven't looked in his face in a long time and he's powerless to stop me from looking deeply into it. He won't be able to tell anyone that I took in every nook and cranny of his actual face and not what it represented to me. He is not a handsome man. He never was. As I take in his features, I wonder why a woman as pretty as my mother ever married him. He is short and has been balding all my life. His toothless mouth continues to make shapes.

You wouldn't be here without him and that's gotta be worth something.

"I guess they took it all from you," I say to myself, eying my father's wilted body and taking him all in. He seems to be looking through me.

I'm running through all the things I might say in this performance. I'm running through all the lines, like I guess the white people and the Black women took it all just like you said they were trying to do. And they finally succeeded. And they took everything you thought you were supposed to be and now here you are. And they wouldn't let you be a man, would they? And that's all you ever wanted.

The director moves in for a close-up of my face.

And I wish you would have tried to be something else. Something more. Because there had to have been something more you wanted to share with the world.

The camera pans out to show me and my father sitting in the tiny plain room of a nursing home. It's the father-son perfect shot. It's the time when I am supposed to lean forward and take his bony hand in mine and tell him how much I love him, which will bring me and the audience to tears. I opt instead to let the clock tick long enough to convince my mother down the hallway that my father and I have had a meaningful goodbye.

I know he loved me. I can feel the power of it taking over the room. He didn't know how to say it or show it, and now his mouth and body don't work. He sacrificed so much of himself to be what he thought a Black man is supposed to be. We sit in silence breathing each other's air until I reckon enough time has passed. I stand and dig my knuckles into my eyes to make them red enough to fool my mother. I don't know why I don't feel much. Maybe I'm just an awful son, but it's far too late to fix things now. I have hidden from him for too long because I know that he'd never approve of who I am, and I never knew who he was. I smooth down my jacket and I head for the door. Just before I walk through it, I turn around to deliver to the audience its final emotional punch. I look directly into the camera.

"I'm sorry I wasn't enough for you."

The director yells "Cut!" and the crew swarms to disassemble the set.

Annette and I grab two drinks and hit the dance floor. I am feeling good. I dance with my hands held up high over my head and a boy with no shirt on comes to dance near me. The cocaine has made me bold and I grab him around the waist, which makes the both of us laugh. I press his sweaty torso against me and land a deep kiss on his lips that he arches his neck to accept. The room is swirling, and I am spilling my drink. The coke has made me start to sniff a little and I can feel my body already asking for more. Annette shouts over the music.

"Do you want me to drive you to see your father?!"

"No! I'll probably just take the bus!"

"Well, just make sure you go! I think you should go!"

I spin around to find the shirtless boy making his way off the dance floor. He gestures for me to follow him. I bet he has cocaine.

I leave Annette spinning on the dance floor and follow him toward the men's room.

A hundred miles away, my father lies alone in a silent room in the last bed that will ever hold him. He stares up at the ceiling unable to speak. He is thinking of me and wondering when I will come to visit. He remembers silencing my squeal when he bought me a *Betta splendens*. He remembers all the things he told me that were for girls. Singing in the choir and spelling bees. He snatches my hand away from its effeminate position on my hip. He thinks back to when he clandestinely removed a small pink shirt from his house in the middle of the night, dropped it in the rusty steel bin out back, and watched it burn as the light from the flames flickered off his face. He recalls the shape of every ball he placed in my hands and the way they all rejected me. He remembers the way his knuckles felt as they struck the side of my face. He remembers all the ways in which he tried to make me act like a man. For my own good.

Shake it off. Be a man. Be more than a man. Be a Black man.

I stand and hoist my suitcase off the seat. I'm getting off at the next stop and my heart is already racing. I will now take another bus to the airport. I will go where James Baldwin lived. Perhaps if I wade in the waters of the Mediterranean where he once bathed, I can absorb some of his strength.

My flight leaves in four hours. I am nervous and afraid and excited. I wonder if, all on my own for the first time, I will feel unfettered. I am afraid to leave American soil but I am excited, for the first time in a long time, to be where I am going. I have booked window seats on all of my flights so that I can rest my head against the window like I like to do. To calm myself, I will pretend that the airplanes are buses. I wrap my arm around my suitcase and pull it close like a lover.

The details and symbols of your life have been deliberately constructed to make you believe what white people say about you. Please try to remember that what they believe, as well as what they do and cause you to endure, does not testify to your inferiority but to their inhumanity and fear.

— JAMES BALDWIN, *The Fire Next Time*

TABULA RASA

Dear Antuan,

I hope that the universe, God, or whatever you may believe beyond this world conspires to somehow place these words in your hands when you are a grown man and I am not too old to remember having written them. My hope, also, is that any nefarious powers that persist in telling Black men and boys who we are or should be have not led you down a road to peril. Because I, at one time or another, believed the lies told to me about such things.

I am writing to you from a beach in Nice, France, along the French Riviera. The day is beautiful. The waters of the Mediterranean sparkle in the deepest shade of blue, and the sky that hovers immense above it is just a few shades lighter. I was surprised to find that the beaches here are not made of sand as they are in America, but rocks. Large ones. I did not bring a blanket, so I am sitting on them with their jagged edges digging into my backside, pen and paper in hand. Yet I have never been more comfortable. The Riviera is busy this time of year and I watch as families and lovers settle themselves, slather each other with oil, and splash around joyously. I hear many different languages being spoken around me, but no one is speaking English. I catch fragments of conversations and their sounds float by me like so many musical notes. I don't understand a word and I don't mind at all. I find it comforting.

I've come here on my very first trip outside of the United States to pay homage to James Baldwin, the intellectual powerhouse and patron saint to Black writers everywhere. I'm renting a room one town over, in Saint Paul de Vence, where he lived and died before I ever knew who he was. He was, like you and me, a Black man who endured the sickness of American racism. He was, like me, a gay man who loved his people. He loved his country too, but he recognized that his country would never love him back. Baldwin spoke, knew who he was, and never allowed anyone to tell him any differently. I am not like him. He didn't seem to need to be loved back and, in this way, he was brave. My biggest failing in this life has been my gasping need to be loved at the expense of so many other things. I have allowed others to tell me who and what I am supposed to be and, when I failed to meet their expectations, I blamed myself. This need to be loved by everyone has led me down dark roads more times than I can tell in one book—in one thousand books even—and all I have to show for it are these stories.

In truth, although Baldwin was brilliant, he is not my favorite writer. But he is my hero. I want to be like him—to drink in his strength, to absorb his dignity and to use it as my own armor. I had at one point convinced myself that he was never afraid, but now I realize that perhaps he was. Perhaps he was afraid all the time and found a way to work through the fear.

I got to Saint Paul de Vence last night, right before a thunderstorm. The sky was that dark blue-black color that sometimes happens ahead of a downpour, and the thunder was looming. A beautiful brown man who picked me up at the airport spoke little English and greeted me with a smile.

"American?" he said in a heavy Arabic accent.

When I nodded my head, his smile widened and he gave America the thumbs-up. I did not have any Arabic or French with which to tell him the truth about America.

He began trying to tell me something as he threw my large suitcase into the back of his hatchback. But we couldn't understand each other, so I nodded in agreement and we rode in silence for a long time until he pulled over to the side of the road and got out just outside the walls of the town. He went to the back of the car and removed my bag. I had no idea what was happening so I got out too. We babbled at each other again until he laid his hand out, palm up. He then placed the tips of his index and middle fingers on his flat palm and walked them across like legs.

From this, I surmised that one cannot simply drive into Saint Paul de Vence. One must walk into the village, as the streets are too narrow for cars. I nodded that I understood and he drove away. The moment he did, the sky opened up and began to dump all of its water. I looked down at my phone and it had gone completely dead.

I stood on the side of the road for a long while with anxiety and fear quickening my heartbeat, until I decided to start walking to find my rooming house. I walked up and down the cobblestone streets in the pouring rain. I found awnings here and there to hide under. I asked a few people who didn't speak English to help me find the street I was looking for. They couldn't. Or wouldn't. An old familiar feeling began to wash over me along with the rain. I wanted to give up. I wanted someone, anyone, to save me. I have spent a lifetime giving up in one way or another. I have believed every person who told me all the things I couldn't and shouldn't do.

So I just walked, listening to the wheels of my suitcase rumble against the cobblestones until I was soaked to the skin. And then a man on a motorbike came speeding up the road and, in an effort to dodge the splash he was going to cause from the puddle in front of me, I leapt around a corner and divine providence took hold.

Right in front of my rooming house.

I had a little trouble with the door code.

But it opened.

I had a little trouble with the key.

But the lock eventually took pity on me.

I was soaked through. It was dark inside my room and I tried the light switch, but the power was out. The Shakespearian thunder rattled the windows as the rain battered them. I was tired and hungry and in a strange medieval village in France, minutes from where James Baldwin lived and far from home. Stranger in a strange land. I sat in the dark with only the occasional lightning strike to illuminate the room and I was grateful. I was thrilled. Not only because I had made it safely inside, but because I had done something I never thought I could do. I had, for a moment in time, overcome the fear and anxiety that has plagued me for most of my life. I didn't need anyone to save me.

One of the reasons I took this trip is to prove to myself that I am allowed to take up space in the world. I used to believe that the space I occupied was conditional. That I had to please anyone and everyone around me in order to exist because I had made the horrible mistake of being different. The other reason I came here is because, lately, I have been thinking about my own death. I used to wish myself dead all the time. I've even tried to bring it about. But I am not thinking about my death like that any longer. Now I worry that my death will come to pass and with my final breath, I will realize that I've allowed my one and only opportunity to live to go to waste. So I have come to France to try to ensure that the feeling of wanting to live fully and unapologetically, like Brother Baldwin did, endures.

Since arriving, I have walked the cobblestoned streets of Saint Paul de Vence and looked out over its battlements and into its verdant mountains and low valleys. The air here feels different than it does back home. I feel the lightness from having a weight lifted from my shoulders that I barely knew that I was carrying. I can breathe. For the first time in my life I feel as though my race doesn't matter and I understand fully why Baldwin came here to live and never looked back.

I have only recently begun to factor my mental health into the act of living. Black life in America doesn't seem to allow for it. As a race, we are often admired for how "strong" we are and for how much we have endured. The truth is that we are no stronger than anyone else. We have endured, but we are only human. It is the expectation of strength, and the constant requirement to summon it, fake it, or die, that is erosive and leads to our emotional undoing.

A long time ago, I witnessed your father training you up. I could tell he subscribed to the belief that the harder a Black man is, the stronger he is and the more fortified he will be to deal with a harsh world. He was teaching you early on that your most tender feelings are your worst enemies and that pain and weakness are the same thing. He was teaching you that masculinity and strength are the same thing. He was teaching you that vulnerability is dangerous.

There is no way that I, someone you've never met, can convince you that this isn't true. I have no method to persuade you that the act of shoving your most tender feelings way down deep or trying somehow to numb them will only result in someone else having to pick up your pieces later. I have wasted time trying to numb myself with drugs and alcohol in ways that made me both vile and pathetic. I know now that I never want to be that person again. All I have are these stories, these cautionary tales of devalorizing one's own life in service to some standard that you are led to believe is bigger than yourself.

I was witness to one of your very first experiences, of someone trying to twist you into a shape of manhood that they believe will protect you. It can be a brutal act, even when wrapped in love. This will be reinforced for the rest of your life. There is no way that I can convince you that you have no obligation to honor these demands. It is only through your own lived experience that you will learn that living on the outside of "normal" provides the perfect view for spotting insecure and flimsy principles camouflaging themselves as leadership or righteousness.

I am exhausted by people telling me how to be Black, how to be a man. I've grown weary of others telling me how to be. And when

I go home, I will try my best to lead the rest of my life the way I'm advising you to, commanding control of my own sovereignty. The pressures are enormous. But I know that I have to try. I hope that you will try as well.

I know it is not my place to tell you that feeling and working through pain and anger is what creates a man. I have no business telling you to be gentler with yourself and with others and to take responsibility for your own shortcomings, not to place them in the hands of others and then stand there waiting for them to repair you. I have only just learned all of these things myself.

But know this, Tuan: it would be a mistake to wait around for anyone to save you. You will have to save yourself. And I hope that you do. I hope that you have.

I hope you have become a man who cries and allows himself to feel all of the emotions, not just anger or desire—a man who sees others' perceptions for what a Black man in America is *supposed* to be, eschews those notions and walks away. Your life belongs to you and no one else. Not white people who do everything in their power to make you and themselves feel as though your life is worth less than theirs, and not Black people who may try to shame you into behaving a certain way.

I hope you are charting your own course, no matter the hardship. But I am not naïve. I know that anti-Blackness exists all over the world, even here in France. And I know that when you can't bring your full emotional self to hardship in a healthy way, life can become challenging.

Others will try to teach you that strength is little more than constantly setting yourself to the task of proving that everyone else is weaker than you. I say that strength is far more than that. It is proving to yourself day after day that you are capable of more than you were yesterday. This is why I have traveled. I needed to see that there was far more to life than these lies.

Back home in the United States, stories of unarmed Black people being murdered abound, most notably by police, but also by white people who are "afraid for their lives." So many white people in America are "afraid for their lives" all the time. Far too many of them seem to prefer being "white" to being human. I hope it will be different for you. I hope things in America are different by the time you read this. My fear is that they won't be.

You can choose to live as a citizen of the world wherever you are. You are entitled to have all the experiences and feelings that come with being alive. Feel them all deeply. And if you happen to find real love, run to it, and give it back fearlessly to the person who has gifted you with it. Your life belongs to you and no one else. The older I get, the truer that feels.

I am in the last half of my life now, not the front half. My death will come sooner than I like, and so now is the time when I want to embrace the parts of my life and the parts of the world that I've missed. I can only hope that it's not too late, because I deserve the full range of human experience and so do you. My heart, in these past few days, has been full of love for humanity. The only difference now is that I am including myself in the process.

I don't know you. I don't know if you have, through no fault of your own, become a symbol for me of every Black boy who is forced to pretend he is someone he isn't.

In the end, all I hope is that you enjoy your life—in your skin and on your own terms, light-years away from the white gaze and all those who seem to believe that you need to justify your life to them.

There is so much more that I wish I could tell you, but there isn't enough paper or ink or time. And there are some things that only your own experiences can teach you.

I will now take off my shoes and walk over these slick, sharp stones into the clear blue water of the Mediterranean. I will look out upon the same waters that Baldwin did when he first came here as a young man so long ago. And where the water is deep, I will lie back and allow it to buoy me up, so that I might look into the vastness of Baldwin's sky. A Black boy from a shitty town in northeastern Ohio floating in the immenseness of the sea.

And, for the first time in my life, the possibilities will seem limitless.

Love,
Brian

ACKNOWLEDGMENTS

I have had much assistance both emotional and technical from many people. Please forgive me if I've left anyone out.

Thanks to all of you for your love, encouraging words, music, jokes, friendship, pettiness, and faith in me: Deesha Philyaw and Yona Harvey for showing me what grace and confidence look like. Madeline Hershey for believing in me from the very beginning. Brian Funk and Tara Cameron for your gift of friendship. I don't know what I'd do without you two. Jason Shavers, Malic Maat, Michael Massie, Rodney Swartz, Alex Fruyzinski, Nathan Bell, Leslie Donovan for your laughter and endurance. Michael Martin and Evelyn Kitchens-Stephens for starting me off on this journey.

Thank you to all those who hung in there with me and continue to do so.

Thank you to my family. My brother for teaching me forgiveness and the importance of family and acceptance. Thank you to my sister for teaching me sensitivity. My auntie Annette who teaches me strength and my cousin Brittany who teaches me kindness.

Thank you to my mother to whom I owe everything.

Much gratitude to the staff at Houghton Mifflin Harcourt for believing in this book, but especially to Rakia Clark, who believed in this project hard enough to push for it and make me want it just as much as she did. Thank you for making me a better writer. To Danielle Chiotti who walked up to me after a performance one night, asked if she could be my agent, and changed my life.

Much love to everyone at Greenbriar Treatment Center and in my addiction support groups for showing me, through example, that I don't have to be the person I was, and who help me every day to try harder to be better. You have helped me in ways that are immeasurable. To Robin for telling me "you don't have to continue to be wretched." Thank you, wherever you are. Thank you to all who have forgiven me for that time in my life and to those who haven't.

Many thanks to my writing instructors at the Community College of Allegheny County, Chatham University, and the University of Pittsburgh.

And, finally, thank you to my father who taught me many lessons he didn't even know he was teaching.

Love to you all.